Dylid d

Hard Knocks
& Soft Spots

PADDY DOHERTY

Hard Knocks
& Soft Spots

EBURY
PRESS

7 9 10 8

This edition published 2013
First published in 2012 by Ebury Press, an imprint of Ebury Publishing
A Random House Group company

The Random House Group Limited Reg. No. 954009

Addresses for companies within the Random House Group can be found at
www.randomhouse.co.uk

A CIP catalogue record for this book is available from the British Library

ISBN 9780091948436

To buy books by your favourite authors and register for offers visit
www.randomhouse.co.uk

Penguin Random House is committed to a sustainable future for
our business, our readers and our planet. This book is made from
Forest Stewardship Council® certified paper.

Printed and bound in Great Britain by Clays Ltd, Elcograf S.p.A.

In memory of Patrick Simey Doherty, David and Andrew.

Contents

Prologue

The entrance to Gorton Cemetery is easy to miss. The graveyard sits at the end of an ordinary-looking road with run-down houses and a few struggling businesses on either side. It looks like many other suburban streets in the north. For me, though, that road is special. It is lined with the history of my people. A journey there is a journey into the past.

The industrial units that scar the landscape behind the burial ground do nothing to stop the cold wind that blows across the graves in this forgotten corner of north Manchester. It might look inhospitable, but it's my sanctuary. I've spent more hours of my life than I care to remember in that place. It is like a magnet that tugs at me in times of need. When it calls I can't resist the urge to go. I've driven for miles on a whim to get there. I've parked up outside in the rain and the dark in the early hours while the world sleeps and scaled the locked, black wrought-iron gates like an intruder in the night to trudge down the path between the graves in the pitch black and kiss the marble head-stone that marks the final resting place of my beloved first-born son; Patrick.

For 16 years I've been going there to visit him and every time I touch the cold, smooth stone of his headstone, my heart breaks. Patrick was my flesh and blood, he was my best friend; a man's man and growing up to be everything I wanted him to be. He was snatched away into the arms of the angels and when I sit by his grave, on the bench his brother, Simey, bought for him, I feel him watching me. He's probably laughing at me saying: 'Come on now, Paddy, pull yourself together.'

In all, I've buried five children in Gorton; Patrick and my daughters Elizabeth, Helen, Mary Bridget and son Mylie. Each one of my babies is marked with a golden angel and a teddy bear. My own blood, sweat and tears stain Patrick's headstone because I dug tons of rusting metal from the ground to raise enough money to pay for it. There is a picture of his beloved Peugeot 405 engraved into it along with Simey's message to his brother, which reads

> In my own words Par, I love you with all my heart and you'll always be my hero. Rest easy my dear brother because I know we'll meet again together in God's keeping and I know he'll ease my pain.

Patrick and my other children are not alone there. They are surrounded by traveller legends. Gorton is a gypsy cemetery. It is where the community in and around Manchester bury their dead. The graves are neatly kept and, when they are freshly dug or there is an anniversary to commemorate, they come to life with flowers, balloons and mementos left for the people underneath. The names engraved on the headstones along Gorton's pathways speak of bloodlines known to travellers across the land: the Wards, the McDonaghs and the Dohertys.

Patrick lies with Old Davey Quinn, the gentle giant who brought me up as his own son and who was one of the only men whose advice I would listen to. He'd quietly tell me if I was keeping bad company and he'd watch out for me during the times when I wasn't looking out for myself.

Just across the pathway from Old Quinn lies Patrick 'Snick' Keily, a bull of a man who fought for fun and became one of the most respected travellers in Manchester. Snick and I didn't always see eye-to-eye but I admired him hugely. If you ever needed someone to show you fair play you would ask for him in your corner. And just across from Snick there is my brother Dudlow. He was a handsome man and a true gentleman.

The earth in the cemetery is full of good people, but in death as in life, travellers are not always welcome. When my Patrick was buried the widow of the man in the grave next to him didn't take kindly to having her husband buried next to him. She complained; I have no idea why. Perhaps it was because we celebrate our dead. Every year on the anniversary of Patrick's death we hold a memorial for him and travellers from far and wide come to pay their respects. It is not a quiet, sombre affair. We are travellers; we pay our respects raucously. Patrick was larger than life when he was alive so why remember him quietly? We celebrate the anniversary of his death in the same way we celebrate funerals, wakes, births and weddings: with passion and meaning. He loved music and we play his favourite CDs at the graveside. We drink toasts to him and, most importantly, we make sure he's never forgotten. But that widow was having none of it, even though I used to put flowers on her husband's grave. It took her two years of complaining but eventually she had her husband dug up and moved. And where did he go? He ended up right next to the pisspot! It seems she must have preferred her dead husband to be buried next to the toilets, rather than my Patrick. At the time it made me angry but I should have known. Along with most of my people I've faced discrimination all my life. We travellers are so close to our families and our extended families because often it feels like family is all we have in a world where we are seen as outsiders.

Patrick's memory and his name live on, as do the names on all the gypsy graves in Gorton. We carry our dead through life with us and when I sit in that graveyard on my own I feel them all around me. When I'm stressed out and messed up I love going there to be with them.

Right next to my Patrick there's a plot of land set aside for me and my wife Roseanne. I bought it when the widow moved her husband. Gorton is where we'll end up, together in death as we have been in life. I should have been put in the ground years ago. I've cheated death many times. And no matter how screwed up I've been in my life, through beatings and bullets I've always found comfort in the knowledge that when I'm finished I'll be nothing on earth but in a grave in Gorton next to my family, and I'll finally be with God, and with my Patrick.

Traveller Life

I was born Paddy Ward on 6 February 1959 in Cheatham Hill in Manchester. My complexion was as black as coal, so much so that people began to doubt my parentage, and for a time it created quite a scandal in our community. Mummy and Daddy were Douglas and Ellen Ward. To everyone who knew him, Douglas went by the name of Dudley. They were Irish gypsy immigrants who moved over to England to raise a family and look for work. Dudley was a proud man and when I was two weeks old I was taken to live with him and Ellen in their two trailers.

From the beginning life meant movement. We stayed mainly on sites in and around Birmingham. The first one I lived on was near Dudley. It was derelict land littered with piles of rubble where the buildings which used to stand on it had been pulled down. In the middle of the wasteland our trailers looked majestic. There could be any number of trailers on a site, depending on its size. Our trailers were Vickers (the best make you could get) and they had chrome panels on the sides, which Ellen kept spotless with chamois leather, and bay windows. Inside, they were more beautiful than any house. The walls were lined with ornate cut glass mirrored cabinets and the surfaces were polished Formica. The fittings and fixtures were all intricate brass and steel. Today's trailers look very plain in comparison.

Dudley and Ellen had a big family already; my older brothers and sisters were our Nelly, our Johnny, our Lily, our Boo, our Bridgie, our Maggie, our Duck, our Kathleen, our Nan, our Dudlow, our Paddy and our Barbara (family are always 'our' or 'my' in my language). Our Tommy came along later. Our Maggie had her own house in Manchester, she was 19 when I was born and she got married when I was just a few years old. I'd sometimes stay with her when we were in the north-west and we had a strong bond.

I was born in a house but I was bred a traveller. Although we were based in Birmingham we moved around the Midlands and beyond and my older siblings would sometimes be with us or sometimes with other family members. Sometimes we'd stay in an area a few weeks, sometimes for just a few days. The momentum of our lives was determined by where the opportunities to earn money were. Daddy went where he could find a living. He owned two trailers: one for him and Mummy and the other for us children; boys in one bed, girls in the other. There was plenty of fighting. Our Lily was a proper tomboy and she would give us boys a hiding when the fancy took her. To her it was a game. She loved beating on the boys.

I was only a youngster but I remember those days with fond nostalgia. Life was hard. There were no creature comforts. It was basic and often it was brutal but there was a lot of love. We called the world outside the traveller sites the 'country'. The people who lived there were 'country folk'. They didn't trust us and consequently we didn't trust them. As a traveller back then you learnt very quickly to hide your heritage.

Dudley was a metal merchant; he'd collect people's scrap and sell it to yards for a profit. He was the original recycler! Each morning as the sun came up he'd get in his old Bedford lorry and head out into the country to make his living. Often I'd go along and help. There was hardly any schooling for gypsies in those days. Traveller children were expected to help their parents. Boys would work with their fathers and girls would stay at home in the trailer with their mothers cleaning and cooking.

I was expected to start work the minute I could reach a letter-box with my hand and drop leaflets through it. At the age of four I would go out with Daddy, riding shotgun in the lorry, and post piles of bills through doors, then knock on them and pick them up the following day in the hope that the person whose house it was had an old cooker or some form of scrap we could take away and sell. It could be back-breaking work. If you wanted something, such as an old stove or copper water tank, you had to lug it onto your lorry. No one ever offered to help.

Mummy would sometimes come with us and she would bring lunch, which was usually a loaf of bread and a chunk of ham. She carried a tin of dried tea with her and at lunchtime she'd send me to knock at a nearby house with our old kettle and ask if I could fill it with water. I'd carry it back to the van where we'd boil it on a fire and have tea and sandwiches.

I wish I could say the country folk were always courteous but more often than not I was looked at like I was vermin. People made no effort to hide their opinions of us. Most country folk thought Irish travellers were dirt. They didn't have to say anything, I knew by the way people looked at me and my family and the way they spoke to us that we were unwelcome outsiders. But I had to ignore the simmering hatred in the eyes that met mine each time I knocked on a door and had to pretend to be very nice and polite, just in case there was an old bit of scrap I could take away.

Farmers were the worst. They didn't hide their contempt and would chase me away off their land. But you had to knock on doors at farms because often they would be the places where the most valuable scrap could be found. Dudley could sell an unwanted item of heavy machinery and make enough to feed the family for several days. So we would find farms and I'd walk up the lane and knock on the door. I could never tell whoever answered I was a traveller. I'd use as few words as possible in the hope that they would not recognise my accent. Once they heard the Irish lilt it would be game over and I'd have to sprint back down the lane to the waiting lorry, often with a well-placed stone sailing past my ears as I ran.

It became nothing to me to lie about my heritage. I look back now and it makes me sad because I am very proud of who I am. It would break my heart to think my own kids would ever have to lie about who they are. As a child I was never ashamed of what I was or who I was but because of the daily prejudices I encountered, it became normal to live a lie. Being discriminated against was part of life and to survive you needed to adapt and that meant camouflaging who you were. Most pubs would have signs outside saying 'no travellers or dogs allowed'. That is how we were thought of: as dogs. I was brought up feeling like a second-class citizen so there wasn't a sudden realisation that the world was unfair and despised travellers. It was always that way.

When a traveller was having a christening or a wedding you couldn't tell any of the guests the details of where and when until the day it was happening because if word got out that it was a traveller function, the party would get barred from the pub or hall or club and the event would get cancelled. That still happens today, but when I was young, often the police would come to keep the gypsies away.

The police were ruthless towards travellers at that time. A policeman would break your face with a slap for fun and you knew you could do nothing about it. One of my first memories is of the sting of the back of a copper's hand. We were in Dudley near Birmingham and I was only around five years old. We were getting towed out. This was a common occurrence.

There were no such things as designated sites back then. If you saw a piece of land that looked suitable, you would pull onto it and stay for as long as you needed or until you were thrown off. The more remote the land you chose, the longer you would get. If we stopped near country folk we could be there for as little as a day; if it was out in the countryside we may get up to a month. The police didn't bother with eviction orders. There was no mains water, so we had to carry our supplies in jerry cans. If the police wanted us off a site quickly they would empty our water supplies, forcing us to move on in search of more. There was no legal process to it in those days. There were no warnings and no chance to have your voice heard. The heavy hand of the law would make sure you never felt secure anywhere. It was normal to get dawn visits. The authorities would come in heavy and hard and break up the camp before anyone was awake. Possessions would usually be smashed in the mayhem and if any of the men dared to question authority, heads would get smashed too. If you didn't comply and hitch up your trailer and move off in minutes, the tractors would come in and move your trailer for you. To limit damage you had to be able to pack up and get out fast.

On this particular occasion the police and the bailiffs arrived at five o'clock in the morning to throw us off the site. I remember the shouting and the gruff voices. Daddy was yelling to us to get up and get into the lorry. I looked out the window through the net curtains and saw an army of uniformed police swarming out of vans which had pulled up around the site.

'Get out, your sort aren't welcome around here. Hitch up and move on or we'll throw you off,' the police were yelling.

In the gloom of dawn I could see them stomping through the tiny camp with truncheons grasped menacingly in gloved hands.

As I ran out of the caravan to get into one of the vehicles I ran straight into the path of a policeman who was walking towards me. He stopped in front of me cool as anything and looked down at me with a sneer of disgust. Then he raised his hand and slapped me across the face. He didn't say a word. He didn't have to. I could feel the hate oozing out of him.

The slap stung, but I'd had much worse from my own parents and even at that young age I knew not to show pain, so I stood there defiantly glaring back at him as he turned and walked off.

I was a Ward, we were a proud family and it would take more than a bully copper to break my will.

You see, beatings were a way of life. They were how we learnt discipline and respect and they were dished out readily by our nearest and dearest. We lived in rough times and it meant everything to instil proper values in children. We were a very close family. Travellers always are, and when one of us cried, the others would feel the pain. When Mummy gave us a flogging we would all know how it felt. And the floggings were fierce. Particularly bad behaviour was dealt with by either broom handle or branch. As I got older I learnt to welcome the broom. It was my friend. A beating with a broom didn't last as long as a beating with a branch because a broomstick is brittle. I knew to crouch in such a way that my spine would take the full force of the blows and within a couple of strikes the wood would usually snap. A broom beating was short and sharp. I'd smile to myself when I heard the snapping sound of the wood giving way across my back because I knew that particular thrashing would be over. The sharp crack was a lovely sound. After a while a broom beating was easy but when I saw Mummy or Daddy reaching up to break a branch from a tree I knew I'd be in for a rough time. Branches were more flexible, they would never break and would leave angry welts on your back. It sounds very harsh and I suppose it was but it was nothing unusual. There was no cruelty meant by it. It was the best discipline you could get, you'd only do things wrong once or twice.

Many things merited a beating: being a rogue, doing something I shouldn't have been doing, back-chatting my elders or telling a lie. Half the time I wouldn't realise I had done something wrong and I was too honest for my own good. Like a fool I'd always own up, even though I knew what the consequences would be. We were children of innocence. It was lovely innocence; I didn't know how to lie.

Although they were hard times, they were also good times. I look back on them now and it seems so innocent and idyllic. We didn't have worries like we have now. We were close, we had each other and we stuck together. In many ways it was the greatest part of my life. Now children live in luxury. They expect everything and get given everything. The childhood I had taught me to be thankful and never to take things for granted.

Life was all the adventure I needed. I went out working in the country most of the day with Daddy and in the early morning and late afternoon and evening there were chores to do. Each one of us children had a job around the camp, whether it was making sure there was water in the churn cans, collecting wood for the fire or cleaning out the stove. No matter how tired you were you knew what you had to get done.

On the road in them days Mummy cooked on what's called a triangle. It was a tripod made of three metal poles which stood over the open fire outside the trailer. There was a big black cast-iron pot suspended in the middle of the triangle. It was called a skeleton pot and dinner would be cooked in that, or in the big black frying pan we had. Food was basic, stews or fry-ups. We ate together sitting around the fire with the warmth of the flames on our faces and the smell of wood smoke in our nostrils.

After dinner Daddy would always sit down and smoke a cigarette and we'd huddle into each other to get warm and to listen to the night's entertainment: the tales. Travellers are good at yarns. Our stories are passed down through generations. Along the way they get embellished and exaggerated until they take on a life of their own. Daddy, Mummy and even my granny Mary Percy were master storytellers. The stories Daddy told were unreal. They were beautiful stories about traveller folklore and about characters larger than life. He'd leave us spellbound with tales about life hawking on the road in Ireland and the colourful company he kept. There would be feuds and battles and schemes to make money. They told stories that reinforced the strong bonds of the community I had been born into. They told of how travellers in Ireland survived the famine by spreading out across the countryside and earning scraps of food from farmers: an egg here, some milk there and maybe some flour from another farm. They would then combine what they had and share the meagre rations out. That's how travellers survived when the folk in the towns and houses perished. They pulled together and helped each other.

And then there would be the fight stories. Traveller fights were legendary. The stories would be based on real events with blow-by-blow accounts. None of the blood and brutality was left out. Fighting was a huge part of traveller life and boys were taught to use their fists at an early age. I used to sit transfixed, my heart pounding as the elders gloried in stories of violence. The final story of the night would be told by Granny.

'Gather round children,' she would beckon. The light of the fire would flicker across her face, illuminating her twinkling eyes.

She would pull her shawl tightly around her shoulders to keep out the chill and we would lean forward into the heat to hear the best stories of the night: the ghost tales. Granny would fix us with a stare.

'There was once a man called Hairy Tom,' she'd begin. 'He had a beautiful head of jet black hair. He was proud of his hair above all else. But Hairy Tom liked to have a drink and one night, when he was mildly drunk, Tom took a wrong turn on the way home and walked over Athy Bridge.'

We'd gasp. Irish traveller children all knew about Athy Bridge. It was in County Kildare in the homeland and legend had it that it was haunted by an old woman. 'Tom staggered across that bridge on the way back from the pub and sitting in the middle of it was an old woman,' Granny would continue. 'She wore rags and her head was covered in a grey shawl.' Granny would pull up her own shawl over her head for ghostly effect.

'The old lady called out Tom's name but Tom knew he couldn't look at her. "Tom," she sang in her otherworldly voice, "Look at me, Tom". He couldn't resist the pull of her voice and slowly he turned towards her as she stood up and un-covered her face...'

By this time I would be transfixed by the story and so scared it didn't matter that my nylon trousers were shrinking up my shins from the heat of the fire. I couldn't move. The story always ended the same. The woman's face was covered by her long, wispy ghost white hair and all Tom could see were her empty eye sockets staring out from under the hair at him. Terrified, he stumbled home where he caught sight of himself in a mirror and realised that his own hair had turned snow white. Scared stiff, we'd scuttle off into the trailer for bed; exhausted from the terror of it all.

Inside there was no heating, just an old wood-burning stove which was lovely and warm when it had a roaring fire in it but which never lasted the night. In the winter, in the early hours when it went out, we would start to feel the icy fingers of cold reach under the sheets and cuddle in close to each other to keep warm. There was enough room for everyone in those bunks.

The outside world was changing fast. It was the swinging sixties and the time of hippies and women's lib. None of that affected us. We lived the same way our people had lived for hundreds of years. The only difference was that instead of horses pulling our trailers, we had vans and lorries.

We never went on family holidays. Our whole life was one big road trip and everything revolved around working, whether on the site or out in the country. Living was hand-to-mouth. There wasn't a monthly wage for the men, they got cash in their hands and the success of the day's endeavours dictated what was put in the pot that night. If it was a bad day, it would be potato soup. A good day would be a chicken or some lamb.

The one day off we did get each week was Sunday. Mummy and Daddy were strict Catholics like all the Irish travellers. On Sunday we had to get up early to go to Mass. We couldn't eat or drink until we had taken communion from the priest and we were not allowed to work unless it was doing chores around the camp. Daddy would always dress in his best shirt and tie. The only other times we really relaxed were Christmas Day, Easter and St Patrick's Day.

Life revolved around church, work and family. And we had family everywhere. In every part of the country we went to there was an uncle or a cousin. There was a lot of love in my life. However, as I got a little older something just didn't seem to fit. I always felt a little bit different. I can't quite describe exactly what it was, but deep in my heart I just knew there was something about me that meant I didn't fit properly within my family. Now and then I'd catch Mummy gazing at me with a strange, sad look in her eyes. Other times I'd walk into their trailer and Mummy and Daddy would suddenly stop talking and seem awkward. I knew they'd been talking about me. I felt disconnected, like something was wrong.

It would take leaving the family I had always known to find out what that was.

2

Country Life

I was six years old when Daddy asked the question that would change my life. I was only young but I could tell by the way he spoke that it was important.

'Do you want to go and stay with our Maggie for a while?'

He was looking at me intently and I couldn't work out what was going on in his mind. But by the way he was asking I knew I didn't have a choice. It wasn't unusual for me to stay with my older sister, but this was the first time that I'd been asked.

I couldn't work out why Mummy and Daddy were making a big deal of it but I knew better than to refuse. Saying no wouldn't have made any difference; I didn't have a choice in where I went at that age. I went where I was told to go.

Maggie was the most loving and caring of all my siblings and she adored me. She treated me as one of her own so I wasn't too bothered about the change of living arrangements. I assumed it would only be for a couple of weeks as it had been in the past.

'If you want me to go, I'll go, Daddy,' I told him.

And that was it. The deal was done. I went to Manchester to stay with Maggie, her husband and my cousins. I arrived holding a bag with all my possessions in. There weren't many. We didn't have lots of toys. I only ever remember one Christmas present from my early childhood, a pair of toy cowboy guns and their own holster.

Maggie was 27 when I went to stay with her. She had been born in Ireland and came over to Britain with Mummy and Daddy when she was seven. Initially they went to Scotland to look for work and then worked their way south down the country before they settled in and around the north-west and the Midlands.

Maggie was a good-looking woman; she was what I'd call a proper woman. She had a big heavy chest on her and had jet black hair. She looked half-Greek or Spanish. In the sun she would go black like me. Gypsies value dark hair and dark skin so Maggie was a handsome lady. I'd always known how to get round her. If I ever wanted to borrow money I'd rest my head on her ample bosom and let her pet me. Then I'd ask to loan a few pence and she'd put her hand down her bra where she kept the money and pull out a note.

Maggie was married to a man called Davey Quinn McDonagh or Old Davey Quinn as he was known. He was six foot tall, a dead ringer for John Wayne, and built like a bear. But Davey Quinn was as gentle as a lamb. He was like a big jelly baby. People called him the gentle giant. He was wise and kind-hearted, and also a very old-fashioned man who had old ways about him. Usually, he was quiet and thoughtful and he didn't like fuss. If there were too many people around and things were getting noisy or boisterous, Davey would often take himself off somewhere else. But when he wanted to, he could light up a room. When he was minded to be sociable everyone wanted to know him in a pub. He had charisma and when he was around you knew it.

Fighting was bred into Irish travellers of that generation but Davey Quinn wasn't a fighting man. If he saw a fight break out he'd get up and walk out. I used to wonder why he would never fight; he would have beaten anyone.

Maggie and Davey Quinn had a family of their own when I went to stay and over the years it was extended further. There was Cathleen, Mary, Martin, Helen, Dudlow, David, Sheila and Margaret, who was the baby. When I went to stay with them in 1965 I was the oldest child.

Things were very different when I went to stay with Maggie because she lived in a flat. Some travellers decide to settle down and move into flats and houses. Trailer life doesn't suit everyone but true travellers will always be travellers in their heart, no matter where they live. Maggie and Davey Quinn were travellers through and through and the Quinn McDonagh family was just as proud of its heritage as the Wards were.

But while Maggie was happy to live in a flat, after a while I began to hate it. Initially the running water and heating was a novelty, but I had never been enclosed in brick walls for a long amount of time before and after a few weeks I felt trapped. It was suffocating, as if the home had grown arms that had wrapped around me and restrained me. I wanted to feel the motion of my trailer in the wind. In the house everything was too solid and stable. Nothing moved.

After a while I told Maggie that I wanted to go home.

She looked at me, eyes glistening with tears, and said simply: 'No, my Paddy, you'll be staying here.'

I didn't understand why I was not allowed to go and why she called me 'my' Paddy. I didn't belong to her and I told her so. She soothed me then and stroked my hair. I was homesick for the trailer and for my mummy and daddy and my brothers and sisters and the freedom of the road.

These exchanges happened often. I told her repeatedly I wanted to go back to Mummy and Daddy and each time Maggie had the same sad look in her eyes. I never intended to upset her but I could not understand why I wasn't allowed to go back home. She always kept me close, as if she was protecting me from something.

Once, a few weeks into what began to feel like my confinement, Daddy came to visit. When I saw him walk through the door my heart leapt. I wasn't one to show my emotions but I ran to him and threw my arms around him.

'I've missed you Daddy,' I breathed.

He looked down at me with a kind, sad smile on his face.

'I've missed you too young Paddy,' he replied, ruffling my scruffy hair with his big hand.

Maggie watched from the hallway and a glance was exchanged between them. There was meaning in that look, but I couldn't work what it was. I was just glad my Daddy had come back. Secretly, I was hoping deep down that he had come back for me.

Maggie put the kettle on while Daddy sat down with me in the sitting room and asked how I was settling in.

'Fine,' I lied. Then, I blurted it out. 'When can I come back and stay with you and Mummy?'

'You can't son,' he explained. 'You have to stay here with my Maggie because my Maggie is very lonesome over you.'

'But I want to go home to you and Mummy,' I implored.

He looked me square in the eyes and said: 'No, son, you stay with Maggie. She'll mind you better because me and Ellen are going away.'

My heart broke with his words. I felt I was being shunned. I was being pushed away from my family and I couldn't understand why. I started to question whether I had done something wrong to make Mummy and Daddy push me away.

He told me not to cry as I started to sniff and my eyes filled up with tears.

'Okay, Daddy,' I whispered. When Daddy said something you obeyed him. There were no ifs and no buts. I felt empty at the time but I had no say in the matter. He walked away through the front door and left me with that familiar anxious gnawing in my stomach and the overbearing feeling that something wasn't quite right. Something had changed for good. However, at that age I trusted and obeyed what the adults said and so I shook it off and stayed where I was.

Dudley and Ellen went away. I didn't have a clue where. I always loved them deeply with all my heart. Travelling was a hard life but with them I had freedom and had my family and then suddenly I was thrown into the world of country people and houses. Although Maggie, Davey Quinn and their children accepted me and treated me like one of the family, I always felt like a bit of an outsider. They never did anything to make me feel that way, and from the day I went to stay with them I was included in everything they did and accepted. But still I had a deep-seated feeling of alienation.

We lived in a block of flats called Heywood House in Manchester and there were lots of travellers living there at the time. It was a community where everyone knew each other and everyone knew each other's business. I shared a room and a bed with Maggie's Martin. He was younger than me but older than his brothers and sisters. It was natural to me to live in over-crowded accommodation. I'd shared a trailer with my brothers and sisters and we'd all slept in the same bed. In the cold winter we'd sleep in our clothes. Some mornings Mummy would come in to wake us, and see us lined up in a row with our heads up each other's jumpers where we'd jostled about to keep warm in the night. It was pure and innocent. At Maggie's worse was to come. After a few months staying she decided it was time for me to go and get educated. I was sent to St Aloysius Junior School. I had never been in a classroom in my life and couldn't read or write. I was years behind the other children and even when I was dressed like all the other pupils in a school uniform it was still widely known that I was a traveller, which made me a target. I was always a small scrawny child and I was easy prey for bullies: both children and teachers. In those days education for travellers was zero. Like all the other country folk I had deal-ings with, the teachers – the adults charged with the responsibility of looking after me and educating me – could barely hide their contempt for me.

'Go and stand in the corner, Ward,' was the most common command I was given. The teachers didn't even try to include me or encourage me. Some days I would spend the entire time either standing in the corner or sitting outside the classroom. I was excluded from most lessons. I wish I could say it was a problem unique to the school I attended but in the late sixties the main-stream education system had no time for travellers. The teachers were ignorant and rude and it didn't take long before I began to despise them. They say the devil hates holy water; well that's how much I came to hate school. The sad thing was that I really wanted to read. I dreamed of being able to pick up a Bible or a newspaper and understand the words printed on them. I always have. But I was never given the chance or the time. Instead I was humiliated. If I had been shown a bit of love, or even tolerance, I might have been more interested, but I wasn't. Each morning I woke with a sick feeling in the pit of my stomach. I didn't want to go and I begged Maggie not to send me but she made me put on my uniform and I knew there would be a beating for me if I didn't. I had been raised to obey adults so there was no chance of me refusing.

In the entire school there was only one teacher who had the time for me. Miss O'Grady was a lovely middle-aged woman who had a kind, caring nature and the ability to look beyond what I was and try and help me with letters and numbers. I used to love it when she was taking class. She would sit down with me and make an effort with me. She had patience and she treated me like a proper human being. She was a warm, good-natured lady while the other teachers were cold like ice. And although they were bad, the bullies were worse. I was an outsider and was relentlessly picked on. It wasn't just one or two bullies, most days it felt as if the whole school was against me. If I did get to sit in class no one would want to sit next to me. The walk to lessons was treacherous. I was punched, slapped and kicked between classrooms. At lunch I would eat alone in silence, except for the times when other pupils walked past me, called me names and slapped me or threw my food onto the floor. In the playground I stood alone or hid. I was called all kinds of names. Because of my dark skin people called me 'black bastard'. That scandal after my birth when people began to question who my father was because of my skin tone followed me and was brought up again and again as a way of goading me.

It was rare for travellers to get schooled at that time. They would come for a few weeks or months and then disappear. I remember two travellers in St Aloysius who were not like true gypsies; they were like country people. They had been brought up in houses. They talked in country accents, not in an Irish brogue like mine. I couldn't understand what they were. They were like mongrels. I would think, 'What's wrong with you, talk properly'. Either they were ashamed of what they were or they had forgotten what they were. I was always the opposite. I knew what I was and I yearned to go back to the way of life I had been born into. Maggie's Martin, the oldest of the family until I arrived, came for a while too and for a few months the bullies had someone else to pick on. I'm ashamed to say it, but I used to be pleased when other gypsies arrived because it meant for a little while they would lay off me a bit. The bullying never stopped but it was shared out between us.

Going to school was worse than getting a beating at home because when I got a beating from Maggie it was over and done with and forgotten, but at school I got a beating in the morning, another at morning break, one at lunch, one at afternoon play-time and finally one on the way home. It never stopped. The teachers weren't stupid. They knew exactly what was going on but they turned a blind eye to it.

At the start it upset me. I never did anything to deserve the treatment I got and it just brought home to me how much injust-ice and prejudice there was against me and my people. After a while, however, I buried my feelings. I brooded and I rebelled. I never did fight back. I was never any good at fighting when I was little and my survival instinct told me that if I had fought back against one bully, I would have incited the wrath of the whole school. Ironically, given how I turned out in later life, the one valuable lesson school did teach me was that you need to choose your battles wisely. As a young boy in a hostile place I learnt that the only way to survive was to show no weakness, take my beat-ings and try to lay low. I blended into the shadows in the corri-dors and kept quiet.

And then, after a few months, I began to skip school altogether. One day a group of older children rounded on me in the playground. There must have been 20 of them and it began with name calling. 'Dirty gypsy', 'stinking tinker', 'black bastard' they spat at me. The whole school seemed to join in and began chanting, I looked around and all I could see was a sea of faces laughing at me. The gang circled me and started to rain kicks and punches down on me. I rolled in a ball on the floor and waited until they got bored. I stayed huddled on the concrete until I heard them walk away. One last kick in the ribs signalled the end of that ordeal and I slowly straightened up and wiped the blood from my nose. It hurt to breathe where I had been kicked in the side. As I brushed myself down I thought 'Why am I bothering to put up with this?' Traveller life was all about moving on to look for better opportunities and in that instant I decided to move on too – straight out of the school gates.

I was terrified that Maggie would find out, not because I was worried about the beating she would give me, but because I didn't want to disappoint her and I didn't want to disobey her. Half-terrified and half-excited I ran to a nearby park and hid out in a copse of trees until it was time to go home. When I walked in through the front door I steeled myself for the telling off. Maggie was busying herself in the kitchen, tidying the benches and putting things away. My stomach was in knots as I leant against the doorframe, silently watching my sister as she worked. Had the school called Maggie when they realised I wasn't in class? Did they tell her that I had played truant? What was I going to say to her?

But when Maggie turned around and saw that I was standing in the doorway, she smiled, came over to me and gave me a big hug and a kiss on the forehead. 'How was your day at school?' she asked.

Could it be possible that Maggie didn't know?

'It was okay,' I lied, looking sheepishly at the ground.

'What lessons did you have then?' she asked.

Was she testing me? My heart was racing. What if she knew

and she was checking to see if I would lie to her? I took a breath. In for a penny, in for a pound, I told myself.

'We had English and Maths, it was boring,' I said.

'Well it might be boring but education is important,' Maggie explained. Then she turned and walked into the kitchen and continued what she was doing. I had got away with it.

A couple of days later I skipped school again, for the entire day. Again I went to stay in the park until home time and again I approached home with trepidation, fearful that my absence had been reported. It had not.

It dawned on me then that no one really cared whether I was in class or not. In fact they were probably glad I wasn't there, so I went in less and less. Most days I would put on my uniform in the morning, kiss Maggie goodbye, go to school and walk straight past the gates. I found different parks to sit in. I believed at that time that all country folk hated travellers, and I was frightened to go anywhere else in case I got caught by the police who were always on the look-out for truants. I also didn't want to get seen by anyone who knew me or my family and who would tell Maggie. Although I was glad to be free of school on the days I bunked off, the downside was the hunger. I never had money to buy food so I wouldn't have lunch. By the time I got home I was famished and often cold and wet.

My plan to get out of school was as simple as it was effective but another of the commitments Maggie set me was much harder to avoid. To her eternal pride I had been made an altar boy at the church next to the school. Like Mummy and Daddy, Maggie was a devout Catholic and she would beam with pride when she attended Mass on a Sunday morning and saw me standing in my starched robes pretending to read the service and sing the hymns.

The church was the one place where travellers were given equal rights and my main job was to assist the priest in the celebration of the liturgy during Mass. I had to set an example to the congregation by active participation in hymns and by responding in the right places to the priest's service. I couldn't sing and I couldn't read so I couldn't follow what was going on. I was supposed to look alert and sit or stand at the appropriate times. It was trial and error to begin with, and I must have appeared a very slow learner, but I soon worked out what I was supposed to do and when I was supposed to do it.

I wore special robes and got to carry the cross and the processional candles, hold the Bible for the priest, fill the jug with water and present the bread, wine, and water to the priest during the preparation of the gifts.

I was so slow at everything and I couldn't tell Maggie that I didn't want to do it because when I saw the look of pride on her face I realised she would be heartbroken if I gave it up. Martin was an altar boy too and he used to play up to the role, acting saintly and sucking up to the priest as if he was a godly boy. But he was the biggest Judas of them all, because as soon as Mass was over and the robes were put away he was back to his naughty ways. Martin was a master schemer. He would always have a plan on the go to make a bit of extra cash on the side. All traveller kids did. On our walk to school, we'd pass a coal yard and Martin found a hole in the wall around the back of it. It was just big enough for him to crawl through. So a few times a week he would get up extra early, scuttle through the hole, fill half a bag of coal (he was too small to carry a full sack) and do his own coal round for cash. My week was mapped out. Monday to Friday I went to school or played truant and Sunday was church followed by a big family dinner that Maggie would make for us all. The real treat was dessert, which was usually jelly or rice pudding and jam. We'd all get together and often later in the afternoon we'd go to visit our cousins, the Oxford Joyces.

I didn't know it at the time, but during these years I was being watched from afar by a man I had never met. The stranger would often arrive at the school gates and watch wistfully through the railings as I skulked around in the playground trying to avoid the bullies. Only once did he speak to me. I don't recall much about it but I remember he called me Patrick, which I thought was strange because I was Paddy Ward. He asked how I was and he gave me some money and some chocolate. There was a sad longing in him and it seemed that he wanted to talk to me more often. But it would be many years before I finally got to meet him properly.

3

Round One

Freedom is the one thing travellers value over all else, and I lived for the summer holidays. Once the final day of school was over, the long hot days of freedom stretched out before me and I felt like I had been released from prison. In the holidays I was free to roam around town with my cousins. I missed moving around from town to town, I missed the excitement of new places and the anticipation of not knowing what the following day would bring.

Traveller life was in my soul. It was what I had been bred into and the longing for the road coursed through my veins. Life in a flat was routine. I knew that at 6.30 a.m. each day I would have to get up. I knew that at 8 a.m. I would have to leave the house and that by 10 a.m. I would either be miserable at school or hiding out in the park. The holidays broke that monotony.

I spent a lot of time with Martin and although we were the nearest in age and had the most in common, there was often friction between us. Looking back now I can understand why. It must have been hard for him as until I arrived he was the oldest child. I was a threat to his authority in the household. In traveller families the oldest sons have the responsibility of being role models for the younger children and in return the younger children look up to their older siblings. With me in the house, Martin's authority was compromised. I didn't care for people's feelings at the time. I was a loner then. The bullying made me withdraw into myself. I had no friends. I always had the feeling I was an outsider; that there was something different about me and nothing about my life made me feel otherwise.

Martin and I would often row and our disagreements sometimes ended in fights. I was no Muhammad Ali but I was bigger than Martin and usually got the better of him, which in turn led to Martin telling Maggie on me and me getting a beating from her. Our sleeping arrangements also meant that we soon had to make up and forget whatever grudge it was we had.

For travellers, life was governed by the seasons. In spring and summer the men would take to the road to look for outdoor work and the boys would often be taken with them. One summer I had the opportunity to go travelling to Scotland with our Duck and her husband Johnny. I couldn't have been happier. The prospect of trailer life filled me with excitement and when Maggie asked me if I wanted to go away for a while I could barely contain myself. I wasn't bothered about hurting her feelings and Maggie was not blind to what was going on. She knew I was unhappy. I never told her about the bullying or that I hated living in a flat. I buried it deep inside and it sat there like a cancer, eating me up and festering. I had become quiet and withdrawn. I didn't have to say anything to Maggie; she instinctively knew that I was having trouble adjusting to life at school and under her roof and she could see how much I missed Mummy and Daddy. She knew a bit of freedom and a change of scenery would do me good.

Initially the plan was to travel for a couple of weeks. I left Maggie's home happier than I had been for a long time. I could see Maggie was upset and she told me she would miss me but I was blind to it. Bullying makes you like that; you become closed off to the world around you and the feelings of others. All I cared about was getting away from country living.

Our Duck and Johnny had sons: Martin, Paddy, Johnny Boy, Dougie and Jimmy Boy. Johnny laid tarmac and summer was his busiest time. The whole family would set off in a trailer, an estate car that one of the older sons would drive, and John's lorry, and journey across the country looking for work. It was an idyllic and nomadic life. They went where the work was and were not tied to a timetable. They travelled as long as the weather allowed them to work and stayed wherever there was a living to be made.

All the boys were expected to help out and there was no exception for me. We'd go in the morning to load the lorry with tarmac and then drive all day looking for driveways and roads to tarmac. We'd be out until the load was finished. It was hot, hard graft and once the lorry was empty we'd have to clean it, wiping it down with diesel. The lorry was John's livelihood and he cared for it like a man cares for a fine woman. Even the engine was cleaned at the end of each day.

Tarmac had a sweet smell, like burnt sugar, and it stuck to your skin and clothes. It became as natural to breathe in as air, and whenever I smell it I get nostalgic for those days. That summer was perfect. Once we had everything all done and clean,

Duck's Martin and me would go and find a nearby swimming baths and we'd splash about for hours then go back to whatever site it was we were staying at and have our dinner before going to sleep in the back of the estate car.

We travelled to Middlesbrough to stay with friends of Duck and John; a couple called Paddy and Margaret Martin. They had a son, Brian. They doted on him like he was a little prince. At that time Paddy was a very rich man. He was very well-to-do and with his money he had built himself a lovely big, wooden, barrel-topped wagon. He had a horse to draw it. It was a classic old-style gypsy home and his pride and joy. He made an identical replica for Brian. Duck's Martin and I soon worked out that if we wanted to stay in that lovely wagon rather than the back of John's estate car we'd have to get friendly with Brian. However, I didn't care much for Brian. He was manicured; he was bred with a silver spoon in his mouth. We, on the other hand, had been dragged up. But out of necessity Brian became our best mate.

'Would you like anything doing for you, Brian?' I'd ask sweetly.

'We're going swimming, Brian,' Martin would say. 'Why don't you come with us?'

Brian happily tagged along and then as the sun began to set, Martin would ask him, 'So, can we stay in the wagon with you tonight?'

But neither Martin nor I could ever keep up the nicey-nicey act for long. Once a day we'd fall out with Brian and end up having a fight with him. Then later in the evening we'd both look at the old estate car and realise what was at stake. I'd start sweet-talking Brian, just to get back in the wagon. I was a sly old fox.

Then in the morning he'd do something to annoy me and I'd give him a couple of slaps. Brian would say, 'You're not sleeping in my wagon tonight, boys' so we'd have to spin him again. It became a pattern that Martin and I got a morbid sense of fun repeating. We became good friends over that summer and in the years since we have become like brothers. Even now I phone him up and tell him if I have problems… and I have had a lot of problems at times! He was the first true friend I had.

During those months travelling we went to Barrow-in-Furness, Newcastle-upon-Tyne, Carlisle and Scotland. It felt as though the world belonged to me and the possibilities were endless. Wherever we were, we used to find a pool and go swimming every Saturday. It was the one place where I could be myself and be a kid for a few hours. I used to love diving from the high boards. I was a thrill-seeker. The other kids would shout: 'Don't do it, Paddy, you'll die!' That was it: once someone said 'don't do it', I would have to do it. My disregard for heights developed into a neat party trick I used to try and impress other children. I would jump off the roofs of houses onto mattresses. I did it all the time. I would climb up the drainpipe on a building, lift myself onto the tiles and leap off. I never injured myself and never went to the hospital. If there was a dare to be done, people would say, 'Paddy will do it' and that would be a challenge. Once I was dared, I'd have to do it. I never knew fear.

After my summer with Duck and Johnny, when it was finally time to return to Maggie's, I went back to Manchester with a heavy heart. The walls of her house seemed more like a prison than ever.

The thought of returning to school to face the bullies left me feeling empty. I wasn't scared. I'd grown up with beatings so physical pain was not something that bothered me. What depressed me was the knowledge that, after being part of a group of kids my age who accepted me, I was returning to the hostility of country living. I buried those feelings deep down again where they stayed and stained my soul with blackness. When you are the victim of bullying you have dark thoughts and it becomes so there is no love in your heart, just anger. I felt more isolated than ever, I felt worthless and I thought no one loved me. I was so messed up I was incapable of loving anyone.

The effects stay with you. Even now I hate bullying more than anything in the world. I can't stand by and watch someone else being picked on; it's a trait that has got me into many fights. I'll always jump in to defend a victim.

Back at school the old pattern continued. From Monday to Friday I would get my beatings three or four times a day or I would skip school altogether. It didn't make me hard. It made me insecure and distant. I felt disconnected, anxious and frustrated.

Davey Quinn must have noticed this worsening of my attitude because when I was 11 he decided to send me and our Martin to the local boxing club. In all the years I was bullied I never fought back. I wasn't any good at fighting so when he told me I was going to learn the art of combat, I approached the opportunity a little cautiously. Although nowadays traveller children start boxing at an early age, when I was young it was rare for children to box in clubs. The fighting was done outside the ring with bare knuckles.

The culture of fighting and violence was (and still is) part of our identity. Sometimes fights would break out on the spur of the moment in pubs and clubs; especially between travellers and country men, but country men back then were not even classed as a real opposition. Fighting traveller men were quick to react to insults and to anyone who questioned their reputation because reputation means everything to a traveller.

Often though, when it was a fight between two travellers, the battles were arranged and monitored. These organised bare-knuckle fights were the way gypsy men sorted out their differences and also the way real fighting men furthered their reputations. Every Sunday morning, in a park behind Heywood House, men from the flats would gather to resolve their problems or just to see who the best was. If two men had argued about something during the week, they would arrange to meet in the park and fight to settle it fair and square. It was like duelling. It was the same up and down the country, quarrels being settled in car parks and fields everywhere.

Children and women were barred from watching these fights (they still are) and Davey Quinn told us to stay away. But Martin and I would sneak off and find a tree to hide behind so we could watch them from a distance. On a good day you could see ten in a morning and I was fascinated by them. At that time, fighting travellers were ruthless but they were fair.

There are rules to bare-knuckle fighting. There are no weapons, boots are taken off and there was no kicking, biting, pinching or gouging. There are no rounds. If a man goes down he's allowed the space to get up. But, the rules about hitting behind the head or in the kidneys aren't enforced like they are in boxing. The fights are refereed by a 'fair play man'; a respected man chosen from the community that each fighter agrees on. The fair play man has to make sure there is no cheating but he has no power to stop a fight. This can only be done by way of knockout, or when one of the fighters 'gives best' to the other, meaning when he surrenders (which is usually after he's been battered to within an inch of his life).

Watching those fights as a kid gave me such a thrill. Blood would flow freely and bones would get broken. It was raw and ugly, but there was a primal beauty to it. You never got closer to the essence of what it meant to be a traveller than when these conflicts took place. Spectators would have side bets with each other. It was done on the quiet and money always had to be shown up front. But the fighters didn't do it for money, they did it for honour. They could bet on themselves and often, if a punter had made a nice few quid on a fight, he'd give the winner a cut as a sign of gratitude. There were no odds; you matched the amount the other person was wagering. It was and still is a fair way of doing things. Only certain travellers would be involved in fighting and they would look to 'best' other gypsy fighters to further their name and reputation.

Davey Quinn wasn't a fighting man but got the idea of sending Martin and me off for some boxing discipline from a friend he worked with, Old Christie Joyce. Christie had eight sons who went to the gym and suggested to Davey that an introduction to amateur boxing would be just what Martin and I needed. The gym was Ardwick Boys Club in Manchester and at the time it was the top boxing gym in the city. It's long since gone but I still vividly remember the scene when I walked in for the first time. The first thing that hit me was the sound: the *rap rap* of the speedballs hitting the wooden boards, the dull slaps of leather gloves against bags and the whistling of skipping ropes. Above the din was the shouting and roaring. It wasn't coming from the boys who were training there; they were silent except for grunts of exertion. The voices belonged to the men who were training the boys. They barked orders like sergeant majors. Martin and I stood staring about us. This was going to be the place where we would learn to be men.

'Who's this then?' said a gruff voice.

Martin and I looked up. Standing before us was an old man with a boxer's face, all broken nose and scarred brows. This was the chief trainer, and his name was Billy Hayes.

'Billy,' Davey Quinn said with a nod to the man, by way of hello. 'I've brought these two boys here for you to train up.'

Billy nodded, a speculative expression on his face as he looked us up and down. 'You here to fight, boys?'

We nodded.

'See this?' Billy took down a long leather skipping rope that was hanging from a hook on the wall next to him. I looked at the rope, it was as thick as my little finger and as supple and brown as the sticks my parents used to beat me with. 'Win, and this stays where it is – on the wall. Lose…' and here Billy gave it a crack, 'and you'll get it across your legs.'

I gulped, and Davey Quinn's hand squeezed my shoulder reassuringly. The message was clear: do whatever it takes to win.

Billy's dead now but in his day he was a great trainer. As I learnt, brutal discipline was his secret. If you lost a fight, Billy took it personally. He would give you a whipping with that skipping rope to remind you that losing hurt. He'd bring that heavy leather rope across your legs and crack your back so you knew next time to train harder and fight harder. Today Billy would have been reported the police no doubt, but the boys in that gym respected him and looked up to him. They knew the consequences of not following the rules and success was bred into them. Billy made sure all his boys were accustomed to pain.

Billy's partner in the gym was a man called Henry. He was a young, fresh-looking fellow and his life was training boys. I don't know why, but he took to me like his own son. He told me later that could see something in me; he could tell I was a troubled soul from the first day I walked in. Henry spent time with me and took it upon himself to train me and teach me the art of fighting.

Like Billy and his rope, Henry had a trademark disciplinary method too. He used to have a metal star on a shoelace and if you did something wrong he'd crack you with it. When Henry walked beside you in the gym, no matter what bit of equipment you were using at the time you'd step up to it on a different level because you knew if you did something wrong you'd get hit with that star. His methods worked. A session in Ardwick gym was the hardest few hours' training you'd ever have.

The gym was full of different bags, speedballs and old leather ropes with lead weights in the handles. In the middle there was a ring. You had to have proper boxing boots to go in and Davey

Quinn bought Martin and me a pair each when we started. From the minute you walked in, there was no talking, just training. Sessions lasted an hour and 20 minutes with no break. We moved between pieces of equipment and the sessions were punctuated by the barks of Billy and Henry, and the sound of the bell that rang every three minutes.

There was no heating. There didn't need to be. By the end of a session sweat was dripping off me, and in the winter my vest would be enveloped in clouds of steam in the cold. After training we were free to get into the shower and only then were we allowed to talk and mess around, but by that time there was no energy left for messing. It was hard and physical. After boxing Martin and me would walk the two miles home and stop for a bag of chips on the way.

I remember well the first time I threw a punch in the gym. Henry helped me to put on my boxing gloves, and as he was lacing them up, he asked, 'Ever been in a fight, boy?'

I shook my head. I wasn't going to tell him about the fights I had been in, the unfair fights where I was set upon by two, three, four or even more boys. They weren't really fights, they were bullying matches, and it was all one-sided.

I think Henry knew that I wasn't telling the whole truth because, having glanced at my face, he said, 'You've got a lot of anger in you. I can see that. That's great, you can use that. Now,' he said, having finished tying up my laces and walking back a few steps, 'throw a punch. Let's see what you can do.'

My arms flailed wildly as I tried to punch the bag. Henry raised his eyebrows and tutted. 'We've got a lot of work to do,' he said. 'You're small, but you're quick, and you've got to make that work to your advantage.'

Henry set about teaching me movement, control and rhythm. At first I would stand square on but he taught me a fighter's stance; sideways with my shoulder to the person or object I was hitting. He taught me how to control my head and how to control my temper. When I stood in front of those bags they were no longer stuffed tubes of leather, they were every bully who had ever called me a name, hit, slapped and kicked me. I had been bottling all my frustrations and anger up for years and there, in that cold, sweaty gym, it all started to come out. It was a release of pent-up aggression and I loved the feeling.

The sessions were physically demanding and I went three times a week in the evenings on Monday, Wednesday and Friday. My favourite day was Wednesday because that was when I got to spar. The only other travellers in the gym were the Joyce boys; Mike, Chris, Joe, Paddy and Jimmy, and they became my sparring partners. Mike and Joe were quality fighters and they could beat us all if they wanted, but we learnt from them. They were skilful fighters and by the way they sized up opponents and looked for weaknesses you could see the true art of the sport when they stepped into the ring. I mainly sparred with Chris and when we stepped into the ring we wanted to kill each other dead. We used to have such heavy sessions, we'd run at each other as soon as the bell went and *bang, bang, bang*, we'd try to knock each other out. Henry would stand in the corner shaking his head. Sparring was supposed to be for learning technique, the punches were meant to be light taps, but many times Chris and I would step of out of the ring badly broken up and then we'd put our arms around each other and laugh. Outside the ring we were friends but the moment we stepped through those ropes we wanted to do damage to each other. Afterwards, we'd get back to training like nothing had happened.

After months in the gym changes started happening to me and within me. I began to fill out. I was no longer scrawny. My weight went up to around nine stone. I was no longer an obvious target for bullies and although I was still excluded and hated at school, the beatings were less frequent. If a bully did start on me, I'd fight back. I found something I thought I would never have: confidence. I no longer tried to blend into the shadows; I held my head up high. My attitude changed. I didn't feel so much like a victim and I started to respect other people. Boxing gave me discipline and morals and an outlet for my frustrations. I could let all my anger out in a controlled environment.

When I started going to the club I was a lost cause. I was introverted and my will was broken. After a few years there I became a confident, polite teenager. The weekly sessions also had the effect of making me and our Martin bond more. We'd look forward to the walks home from the club and would mess around and get into mischief on the way.

I became so confident in the ring that I would always pick the biggest boys to spar with. Right from the start of my boxing days I always fought kids much older than I was. I have never been tall but I'd always choose to go up against someone who had a greater physical advantage over me because I figured that way I would learn more. My tolerance to pain, built up through beatings from family and bullies, meant it never bothered me to get battered. If I got knocked down three times by one opponent I'd train harder so the next time I only got knocked down twice. To me, that was progress.

I had my first proper competitive boxing fight when I was in my early teens. It was in a smoky community hall in town. There was no glamour; there weren't even tables for spectators to sit at, just folded seats placed around the ring. On that night there were around ten different bouts that varied between three and six rounds, depending on the age and experience of the fighters. There were several different boxing divisions around the north-east and a fighter would be entered into a division depending on the club he trained at and the weight he fought at. The best ones from each division would then be entered into the National Amateur Boxing Association competitions. The idea was that young fighters would box against opponents of similar age, weight and experience.

I soon learnt, however, that the rules and regulations governing these types of amateur fights were not always rigidly enforced. I was a first time rookie and on that night I should have been fighting someone of similar experience. Instead, my opponent was a two-time ABA champion. He was bigger and better and had far more experience than me. I laugh now when I think about it. The rules of fair play didn't come into the equation back then. Names were drawn out of a hat and you fought who you were told to fight.

I walked through the rowdy crowd to the ring without fanfare. Henry was with me. He was going to be my corner man and by the way he was holding his first-aid kit he was expecting injuries to patch up – there were no headguards involved. When I saw the man behind the ropes waiting to clobber me I turned to Henry and asked: 'Are you fighting him or me?' The more I was training the more I realised I could use my hands to good effect in the ring, so even though my opponent looked bigger, I was confident I could take him. I was a traveller. Defeat was not an option.

Before I stepped into the ring I noticed all the ribbons tied to my opponent's trunks. I didn't know it at the time but they were awards for the fights he had won.

I asked Henry: 'What are all those badges on his shorts for?'

'Don't worry about it, they're just decorations.' Henry laughed nervously. 'He's all yours, Paddy.'

My opponent was a man called Bobby McKenley. He was mixed race, several years older than me and several inches bigger all round. He was a proper experienced boxer. Strangely, although alarm bells should have been ringing in my head, I felt excited. The adrenaline was pumping through me and I just wanted to get in that ring and punch the head off him.

At the first bell I ran out of my corner like I had so many times before when I went to spar with Chris Joyce and lunged at McKenley. He side-stepped my right hook deftly and pole-axed me with a straight left to the temple. I felt the room sway a little and grabbed him to buy myself some time until the room swam back into focus. I knew I was in for a tough fight and after the first exchanges, where my punches glanced off him and his caught me square on target, instinct began to take over. The fight became a damage-limitation exercise but although McKenley landed some heavy blows, he didn't manage to knock me down. When the final bell rang I was still standing. It was an easy fight to score for the judges; McKenley won by a unanimous decision, as I knew in my heart he would. I was far outclassed and although managing to stay upright was a small victory and I wasn't bruised or cut, the injuries were on the inside. I hated losing and the thought of it ate at me. I cried like a baby that night and I vowed I would fight him again.

A few months later I got my chance at another exhibition bout. I couldn't wait to get back in the ring and in my heart I knew I would beat him. Once again he beat me. But that time he won by a split decision. I was improving. Defeat hurt as acutely as it had the first time but I knew if I kept getting better I would beat him. It was 20 years until I met him again. By that time my boxing career had progressed to bare-knuckle fighting. We ran into each other in a club and shook hands, two old adversaries who had long since buried the hatchet. There was no animosity at all. We joked about the past and I said to Bobby: 'It would be a different fight now you know.' He laughed and agreed. We both knew if it came to a street fight we'd beat each other's brains in because neither of us was the type to give in.

After my first defeats in the ring as a teenager I trained harder and my confidence and ability as a fighter continued to grow. I began fighting outside the ring, usually with country kids.

Two of Martin's younger brothers, our David and our Dudlow, had started secondary school and when one came home with a black eye I knew immediately that he had been bullied. He didn't have to say anything; I could see it in his eyes. There was no way I was going to stand by and watch him suffer in the same way I had so I hatched a plan with our Martin.

'We'll go to the school, find the cock of the school and the second cock and beat them,' I told Martin.

The 'cock' was the top boy; the strongest and hardest. Every school had one.

'Why have I got to fight anyone?' asked Martin. 'And what if the cock isn't the one doing the bullying?'

My reasoning was simple. Why waste time finding a single bully? In my bitter experience, once pupils in a school identified a victim the whole school would bully him. Every school has a child that all the others pick on. It happened when I was a lad and it still happens today. I figured that the best way to stop my cousins becoming the school whipping boys was to send a message to the whole school, not just a single pupil.

Martin and me arrived at the school gates and soon identified the cock and his lieutenant. Without any explanation I battered him until he was begging me to stop. A crowd gathered round to watch and when I was finished I told them that if anyone laid a finger on any of the McDonagh brothers they would have me to answer to. When they walked through the gates the next day, David and Dudlow were treated like royalty.

My fortunes were changing at school too. My attendance, or lack of it, had not been entirely ignored. I had been excluded and sent to a new school. The mainstream education system had washed its hands of me altogether. Instead I was sent off to a school called St John Vianney in Manchester. It was a Catholic school for troubled children and on my first day there I thought I had walked into paradise.

'You must be Paddy Ward,' said the friendly teacher when I walked into class.

I blinked in confusion. Where was the open hostility? Why wasn't I being sent into the corner? The education system had never treated me as an individual before.

'Come in,' continued the teacher, 'sit over there.'

I sat next to another boy and he smiled at me. There was no hate in his eyes.

I discovered there were other travellers in the school and that the teachers had no prejudices towards us. They treated all the pupils the same – as human beings. Nearly everyone there couldn't read, or some could read and they couldn't write. It was for kids who had been let down by the education system, kids like me. Some of the pupils were wild. They had mental health issues, which they couldn't help and the school understood that. The teachers had a way of controlling the unruly ones that didn't include violence or punishment.

On my first day at lunchtime I was encouraged to sit down and eat with the other children. No one shunned me. It was the first time I had sat in a school canteen and talked to other kids. No one judged me and no one took any notice of my accent. In lessons the teachers spent time sitting with me, talking to me and listening. I felt a kind of warmth that I had been missing in all my previous years at school. I enjoyed the school so much I hardly got into any fights there.

I got to St John Vianney too late and that saddens me now. I was 15 when I first went there and at that age a traveller is a man. As far as I was concerned I was grown up and no longer in need of school. A few years earlier and perhaps I would have been able to read and write. I tried, and I enjoyed the opportunity, but I was set in my ways and I just wanted to get out and work and earn a living. I had outgrown school. I stayed there for a year and I enjoyed every day. There was just one teacher who was bad to me. And I could handle that. Like all the others I had come across in my previous school he was full of prejudice against travellers. I remember him pulling me aside in woodwork class one day and telling me: 'Ward, you'll come to no good, you'll go nowhere in life.'

His words stuck with me. He wasn't the first person or the last to look down on me but I never forgot what he had said. Rather than upset me, the words spurred me on, along with all the other negativity and intolerance that had been directed at me.

4

Becoming a Doherty

Sweat was pouring off me. I could feel it trickle down my forehead and into my eyes. Surrounding me was a crowd, baying for blood, but their voices seemed to come from a great distance, and I locked my gaze onto the eyes of my opponent. We were circling each other, but I could see that he was getting tired. He was bigger than me, and stronger, but I had something he lacked: the hunger to win and the technique to do it.

He had landed a couple of blows to my head and I could feel a swelling in my left cheek. I, only the other hand, had opened a cut on his eyebrow, and blood was streaming down the side of his cheek. I was in better shape than he was, but not by much.

Suddenly he came at me, swinging a roundhouse punch that I easily dodged, and in return I landed a blow to his ribs. I heard a pop as a bone broke. He instinctively dropped his arm to protect his side and exposed his face in the process, and from that moment the fight was mine. Throwing my whole weight behind my right hand, I sent an uppercut to his jaw, knocking him backwards. I followed up with a left hook, and he fell to the ground.

The whistle blew and the referee held my hand up in the air. I had won my first fight.

'And then what happened?' Davey Quinn said, a grin plastered all over his big face.

'I got cleaned up and came home,' I said.

Truth be told, I couldn't wait to go home and tell Davey Quinn that I had won. That feeling when the referee raised my hand in victory... it was a mixture of power and achievement and as potent as a drug. It was tangible proof that I was good at something, and as I gave Davey Quinn a blow-by-blow account of the fight the twinkle of pride in his eyes swelled my chest.

Old Davey Quinn was a wise man. He knew from the beginning that the discipline of the club would help sort out my head and up to a point it had. I had taken to the sport like a duck to water. After my initial clumsiness the skill of fighting was coming naturally to me. I fought orthodox, which meant I led with my right hand. I loved the uppercut; the punch that sliced upward. You could put everything behind it, every part of your body, every ounce of aggression, and when an uppercut connected with a chin, it would jerk your opponent's head back, leaving it an open target for a hook to the side of the head. I was small so I fought inside my opponent's reach, I got up close and in their faces. I didn't have the reach to stand back so I took the fight to them. When I was fighting, the aim wasn't to score points or show finesse, it was to severely hurt my opponents. I just wanted war. At that time I believed that the whole world was against me. It wasn't, of course, but I was young, I'd had a messed-up life up to that point and I was angry. When I tasted victory I didn't just beat an opponent, I beat my life and all the troubles in my head. There was nothing sporting about it, it was messy. All I wanted to do was hurt. I felt no guilt when I inflicted pain. The club taught me skill and technique and discipline but I ran on pure aggression.

At the time there was a boxer called 'Gypsy' John Frankham who became the British middleweight champion in the early seventies. He was a traveller but he was also famous outside traveller circles, and that was very rare. He was my hero and a hero to many traveller boys. He was the man I wanted to be. I remember watching him fight another boxer – Chris Finnegan – for the title. I was with Davey Quinn, Martin and the other children at home. It was a rare treat to be allowed to watch television with the adults and when Frankham stepped in the ring and was announced as Gypsy John Frankham it was a proud moment because in those days when people knew you were a traveller you weren't going anywhere. Most of us knew to hide our heritage if we wanted something from country folk. All us travellers knew how hard it must have been for Gypsy John to have made it into the world of professional boxing because the sport then was heavily prejudiced against travellers.

Even so, I knew no matter how good I was, I wasn't going anywhere in the ABA championships because I was a gypsy. I was robbed of decisions by judges all the time. I had beaten so many opponents and lost on judges' decisions that I knew in order to win I would have to knock someone out or damage him so badly the fight would be stopped. Even on a schoolboy level it was corrupt and discriminatory.

Fighting was a big part of the male traveller tradition so it was doubly hard for us to be excluded from boxing. We loved fighting and wanted to be involved. Johnny Frankham worked so hard to get where he did because he had so much more to prove and he changed a lot of things for travellers. In the years since more and more traveller boys have joined boxing clubs. In my time I entered the ABAs but the odds were always against me. I got to the quarter-finals comfortably but was stonewalled from going further by crooked judges.

There was no effort made to hide the discrimination. Even at larger events the judges would pass ridiculous decisions and it was obvious to everyone what was going on. But because there were travellers involved, no one ever questioned the results. Ardwick entered one bout against a rival club from Liverpool. As we were a club from Manchester against a club from Liverpool it was a real grudge match. The Ardwick team was composed of me, our Martin, Mike, Joe, Chris Joyce and a boy called Mark Bates. Mark was the only non-traveller. We all won our bouts easily, but at the end of each fight the ringside judges awarded the points to the other side. It was embarrassing and as obvious as the nose on your face. Mark Bates took his decision in good faith but the rest of us knew what was happening and at each decision we protested loudly. The Liverpool boys knew they were beaten fairly and squarely but did nothing to challenge the decisions and instead slunk off to their dressing room. I was used to the injustice but what annoyed me more was the fact that those boys made no effort to right what was an obvious wrong. We knew there was only one way to get justice, and when we left the hall where the tournament was being held we went to find the Liverpool boys in their changing room. The six of us barged in and I locked the door behind us so no one could get out. Then we set about getting our revenge. With gloves off us we meted out some good old-fashioned gypsy justice and beat the living crap out of the other boys. They ran off to the officials bloodied and bruised and Ardwick got banned from entering contests across the whole country for six months. The incident even made the national boxing magazine, under the headline 'Gypsy Team Runs Riot'. Billy Hayes went mad and the rope was dished out to all of us but we didn't care. We had made a stand.

My reputation as a hard man was growing outside of the ring too. We lived in a tough area and Davey Quinn was a quiet man so it fell on me and Martin to protect the honour and reputation of our family. I would get into fights with men much older than myself. At 14 and 15, I'd often find myself involved in spur of the moment scraps with men in their twenties.

During my teenage years I had a love/hate relationship with Martin. I hung around with him more and more and although we loved each other, often he would get on my nerves. Because he was a few years younger I couldn't beat him up so I had to come up with other ways of getting him back when he riled me. He won't mind me saying this but when he was younger he was one arrogant little kid. He went through a phase where he used to have his head shaved like Kojak's. That's what we used to call him. He was so cocky, he was the first traveller to shave his head bald and he used to go round with a lollipop in his mouth. Even today he's still known as Kojak. He used to be everything in the boxing gym, prancing around like the cock, and he was nothing to look at but he had a punch that would stop a man dead. One day we had been arguing about something and I vowed to get him. Old Quinn and Maggie spoilt him rotten and I wanted to put him in his place.

In the neighbourhood there was a Greek chap called Christos. He was a big lad Martin's age and he was a hard case with a reputation as a fighter. He also owed me five pounds, which in them days was a lot of money for a young teenager. I had given Christos a couple of hidings in the past so he was frightened of me. When I called on him to demand my money, which he handed over, I could see the fear in his eyes. That's when I had the idea. You see, he didn't like Martin either but he would never lay a finger on Martin because he was too scared of me.

I stood on his doorstep and started scheming.

'Would you like to beat our Martin?' I asked him.

'Of course I would, Paddy,' he replied, 'but you'll beat me if I do.'

'I'll tell you what, Christos,' I said, putting an arm around him. 'I give you permission to beat Martin. You do it properly and give him a good beating and I promise I won't touch you… and you can keep the five pounds.'

Christos couldn't believe his luck. He was being given the green light to fight our Martin and he was going to get paid for the pleasure. He nodded his head eagerly as I handed him back the crisp note. I had just put a £5 hit out on my cousin. In those days we all had schemes to make money and we kept the spoils hidden from our parents. I got in on Martin's coal scam and took scrap where I could find it. I went out working with Quinn and he would give me a fiver a day. I was also becoming proficient at getting into cars and stealing cassette stereos to order. I was a genius for getting into cars. I hid my money in a sock and Martin had his stashed under a stone at the front of the flats. I was always careful with money and saved it. Martin on the other hand would go to the youth dance and blow his on Vimto and cakes for his mates.

I told Christos where he would be able to find Martin and told him to go and do it there and then. He walked off like He-Man. But my plan backfired spectacularly. Christos found Martin and ran into him all guns blazing. Martin coolly dodged him and fought back better and harder. Christos went down on the concrete and as Martin was punching him the face he started to whimper: 'Please don't hit me any more. Paddy made me do it, he paid me to beat you.'

'How much did he pay?' Martin asked.

Christos told him and took the money out his pocket to show him. Martin snatched it off him, gave him one final crack and went home to tell Maggie that I had paid a boy to beat him up.

'Where is the fiver now?' Maggie asked.

Martin lied that it had gone and when I got home Maggie gave me a beating. I'd lost my five pounds, I got a beating and more importantly, Martin had won.

Home life was a mix of ups and downs. I'd often get a beating for doing something wrong but there was a lot of love too and Maggie, who dished out the punishment, was only trying to do right by me.

I remember when I got my first tattoo. It wasn't a professional job at all – it was done with a needle and some ink in the playground behind Heywood House by a boy called Clyde who later became my brother-in-law. I'd wanted one for ages – all the men that I admired showed off their biceps with skin art, and I wanted to be part of it.

I decided to get a tattoo of a bird. It was a long, painstaking process. Clyde had a needle and a bottle of Indian ink and spent hours jabbing at my arm. All the way through I was saying 'What's it looking like?' and the answer was always 'It's looking good, Paddy, you're going to love it.'

When it was finished Clyde leaned back proudly and admired his handiwork. I twisted my arm to get a better look.

'It's good eh Paddy?' he beamed.

For a moment I couldn't speak. 'W-what's that supposed to be?' I stammered. What I saw looked less like a bird than a pile of bird shit. I looked at Clyde. He gave me a weak smile.

'You've messed my arm up for life!' I roared, and laid into him. To be fair on him, he took his beating. He knew that he'd done a piss-poor job.

I got a beating in turn when Maggie saw what I had done. 'What in God's name is this?' she cried. It was a stick beating, I got two belts and the stick snapped so I wasn't too upset. I was more worried about the tattoo, which I later had covered over.

Maggie's house was home. Periodically in the holidays I would go off with relatives but Maggie's was my main base. I was close to Maggie as her brother but I never had in my life what most people see as traditional mother and father roles. I thought I had it with Mummy and Daddy but that got taken away when I was six. They still came in and out of my life but I had given up asking to go back and live with them. I had missed out on that parental bond and I felt abandoned and confused, which made me angry and frustrated. But Maggie and Davey Quinn were good people and they looked after me as their own. Davey Quinn would always call me 'son' but I recall once he took me aside and said: 'Paddy, son, you do know I'm not your real father, don't you?' I did but Old Quinn was the closest to a father figure I had.

I would go out working with him tarmacking in the summer. We'd hawk tar together, looking for houses that needed work. They were lovely days. It was an honour to hawk with Davey Quinn. I still tell my children about those days even now. I loved everything: digging out, filling the barrow, wheeling the barrow, raking and rolling. I used to want to do the whole job myself with no help. I liked it because it was physical work. Davey would offer to get a labourer but I refused. I didn't want anyone, I would be drowning with sweat but I loved it. Me and Quinn did that for years. We started every day at 7 a.m., we got the tarmac from a yard in Old Trafford and we wouldn't finish until the load had gone late in the evening. I miss those days.

I loved all my family but I wasn't in love with them. There is a difference. I didn't know what that deep family love between a child and its parents was because I never had it and I missed it. I would have loved to see what it was like to grow up in a normal household where I knew who was who. You see, all through my childhood I had the feeling that something was amiss. I moved from person to person and my foundations were never settled.

Traveller children idolise their parents and their parents idolise them in return. Traveller boys worship their fathers and adore their mothers. I saw it all around me in my cousins and brothers. But I never had that one single male figure and one single female figure to attach all my attention to.

As I grew older I started to realise that there was something about me that was being kept from me. I would catch the tail end of conversations. I would wonder why people would call me bastard, I was called that many times, and I would catch names – 'Patrick', 'Simey', 'Doherty'. They were whispered behind my back or I would be ushered out the room when they were mentioned. I started to doubt the story that had been told to me about who I was and where I was from.

In the end there was no one moment when I realised Mummy and Daddy were not my real mother and father. Everything just fell into place like a jigsaw when I was in my teens. I heard a bit from here and a bit from there. I had known there was something not quite right since I could remember but eventually I realised that Maggie was not my sister, she was my mother and her children were not my cousins, they were my siblings.

It had always been kept a secret because Maggie had me when she was young and unmarried and people thought I was black. In them days that all amounted to sin, and her mother and father, Mummy and Daddy, took me to raise me. It wasn't something people talked about. It was seen as the family shame. But when Maggie got married and settled with Davey Quinn she wanted me back and Dudley and Ellen couldn't refuse. The people I thought were my parents were my grandparents.

By the time I was 14 or 15 I had worked all this out. The pieces of the jigsaw were finally in place, but completing the puzzle did not give me the peace I thought it would. I knew the reason for my feelings of alienation, but they still remained. And they were joined by an uneasy sense of confusion. I'd been lied to by my real mother and I couldn't switch off the feelings I had for Mummy. I felt betrayed.

To understand why I never raised it as an issue with everyone involved you need to understand traveller families. They are loving and kind but secretive. Their secrets are buried and shame is never dug up. Travellers can be very ignorant like that, they don't talk.

Even when Maggie knew I knew her secret she didn't tell me what my name was, the name of my father. In turn, I never called her 'Mother' until years later. I always wondered who my real dad was. I would go visiting relatives and they would say 'you are the picture of your father', and then someone would change the subject. I adored Daddy and I adored Davey Quinn. They were the two big male influences in my life up to that point. But once the truth was out there was another man looming large in my life and he was a complete stranger: a shadowy figure on the edge of my imagination. Who was he? I tried to ask but I learnt very quickly that discussions about my father were out of bounds. I would be left in the dark. His identity was hidden from me. I often wondered if I would ever meet him. Family is so important in traveller life and gypsies carry their heritage through life with them. You wear your family name like a badge of honour; especially traveller men. Daughters get married and lose their names but sons never do, they carry your name forward. Without a father I had no identity. I didn't know who I was or what I was and it seemed to me that I would never find out.

I was beginning to lose hope. I had heard the name Simey Doherty mentioned quietly on many occasions through my life and I knew there was a link. I knew of only one Simey Doherty. He was a legendary fighter; a brutal man with a fierce reputation among travellers. I never put two and two together. But all that changed at a chance meeting in a dance hall in Bolton.

It was a Saturday night. Dances were where young travellers would go to meet girls. There were only a few in the area that allowed travellers in. These were still days when pubs would have signs on barring us from entry so any venue that welcomed us would be well attended.

I was with the Joyces that night. I didn't dance, it wasn't what young men did. I was standing at the side of the dance floor when a man came over to me, put his arms around me and kissed my cheek.

'Hello Patrick,' he shouted over the music.

Normally I would have hit a man who did that to me but the guy seemed so friendly and pleased to see me I couldn't help but laugh.

'My name is Paddy, not Patrick,' I told him.

'No,' he said. 'You are Patrick Doherty.'

'I'm Paddy Ward…' I began. But then the penny dropped. This man knew my father.

He explained that his brother was Simey Doherty, the name I had heard whispered on several occasions as I grew up, and that Simey was my father.

'I'm your uncle Francey,' he said putting his arm around me again. I was gobsmacked. It was the first time I had ever met someone who knew who I really was and who knew my father.

After that the questions came thick and fast. Who was he, what was he, where was he. I discovered that Simey was the same Simey Doherty I knew of, he was a well-to-do man who moved around the country but spent a lot of time in the West Country. He had a family of his own and he was a legendary prizefighter. I listened slack-jawed as my history was revealed to me.

Francey told me that he had only decided to go to the dance at the last minute and that when he spotted me he knew who I was because I looked just like my dad. He was as shocked as me. I was the last person he expected to see there.

'You're a Doherty, too,' Francey explained. 'It's a proud name to carry.'

I knew he was right. I had heard about the Doherty fighting tradition.

'Why did my father never make contact?' I asked.

'He did,' explained Francey. 'Whenever he was in the north-west he would come to your school and watch you from a distance to make sure you were okay. He could never approach or speak to you because it would not have been right. But you are older now, it's time you met your father.'

And that's what happened. By another quirk of fate my father was staying in Liverpool and Francey told me to meet him the following day so he could take me to him.

I met Francey at a trailer site just outside the city. I was nervous and excited. Finally all the pieces would be slotted together. I was also defensive. Years of not really fitting in had made me distant. It was a survival instinct and I still harboured resentment towards my father and mother for the lie I had been spun all my life. But curiosity won out: more than anything I wanted to know what my real heritage was. In the trailer I met my granny, Old Aunt Jane.

I was Simey's first-born and that made me the most important member of his family, and so Aunt Jane worshipped me the first time I met her. She was lovely, like an old fox. She had a head of ringlets and her skin was pure pink. She had a big family to look after and a hard life, but you could see she looked after herself. Aunt Jane always wore a bib over her clothes like all old traveller women did back then, and she was cosy, just someone you would naturally want a cuddle from. Her trailer was beautiful inside and out. It was a four-wheel Jubilee trailer and it was all cut glass mirrors, baskets of grapes and fruit engraved in the glass.

'You're the picture of your father,' she crowed.

Then we went to a pub where Francey had arranged to meet my old man. I was only drinking orange. I didn't drink at the time but while I was waiting nervously I wished I had a whisky.

Ten minutes later, a man walked into the pub. He was short, but powerfully built, and he looked like he knew his way around a fight. I saw how the other people in the room looked at him, with respect. This man was dark, like me, and he had a brooding quality about him that felt quite intimidating to me at the time. It was my father, of course, I knew it had to be him the moment he walked in the door, and I could feel my spine tingle as he walked towards our table.

'Hello, Patrick,' he said in his Irish lilt.

I wish I could say there was an instant spark but I would be lying. We were like strangers, our paths had never crossed and I'd never seen a picture of him. So we just got talking like two men.

It was only when his sons, my brothers Johnny, Charlie and Hughie, came in that emotions started to overflow. Charlie was only a little boy, he was coal black with curly hair and I lifted him up. He put his arms around my neck, kissed me and said 'I love you, Patrick, I love you'. Hughie and Johnny put their arms around my waist and said, 'You're our big brother now.' I started crying then.

Hughie wanted me to go back and live with them there and then.

'Let's bring him home,' he said to Simey.

'I can't,' I said.

The old fella knew I had things to sort out before I could think about staying with my newfound family. 'He'll come to us,' he said to his sons.

I stayed in the pub for a couple of hours with them and over the following months I saw them regularly until my father went travelling back down south. I couldn't see the resemblance between me and my dad. Everyone said there was. Even now people say it and although I still don't see a striking resemblance I do sometimes catch myself saying something or carrying myself in a certain way and think, 'Fuck me, I'm getting like the old fellow.' It's the way I stand, the way I walk. I can't help it; it's like he's got hold of me. Over the years we have got into loads of arguments because we are so much alike. All my other brothers will back down but me and him don't, we front each other. We get drunk together sometimes and he'll say, 'You know, Patrick, you are more like me than anyone in the world, you are every vein in my body.' I'll swear blind I am not but in my heart I know I am. I knew from the moment I met him I was a Doherty and I would have loved that love between a father and son when I was growing up. I was always looking for that proper father-and-son bond, even though I was close to all the other men in my life. I never had that blood bond until I met the old man.

The gradual realisation that I was Maggie's son and that her children were my siblings and not my cousins shook the very core of our home. It must have been particularly hard for our Martin and initially we both struggled with the fact that we were brothers, not cousins. The whole axis of our relationship had shifted. In one of our regular fights we cleared the air. It happened one day when Martin had done something to annoy me. I've long since forgotten what.

We were in the fields at the back of the flats and I'd had enough. I shoved Martin hard in the chest. As a youngster I never swore. No traveller child did. It was a big scandal if a child was heard to swear in those days, unlike now where cussing is seen as normal in many traveller families. But by that time I was 16 and I had started to develop quite a taste for cuss words.

'Fuck off you bastard,' I spat at Martin. 'I never asked to be your brother. We've grown up together and you've never looked at me as your brother and you've never treated me as your brother.'

I pushed him again and he stumbled back. He regained his balance and came for me.

'I was the oldest before you came along and ruined it Paddy,' he sneered before he swung. His fist landed on my jaw. I countered and we stood toe-to-toe and unloaded all our resentments. We battled until we had nothing left and it sounds strange but it cleared the air. Neither of us backed down. Martin wanted me to know that I wasn't better than him, he was Old Quinn's oldest son and then I came in and pushed him to the side. He was always spoilt. He thought I was going to be the best. Davey Quinn loved me, he truly did with all his heart, but Martin had a place in his father's heart that I could never take.

We understood each other better than ever after that fight and it was on that day that we truly did become brothers. We had always been close in a love/hate way. But after that fight we just accepted each other's place in the mixed-up family we lived in.

5

Daddy's Boy

Our home had been shaken by an earthquake. The name 'Doherty' hung in the air and I felt stuck in the middle with my confusion. I was Maggie's son as plain as day but I couldn't bring myself to call her 'Mum', that name was still reserved for Ellen Ward. The knowledge of who I actually was led to more questions. Why had I been fed secrets all my life? Why didn't my father ever make contact with me as I was growing up? Part of me was relieved that the facts were now out in the open but I still felt empty and let down. I had missed out on so much and the people I trusted had lied to me all my life. Simmering resentment was burning a hole in my heart. I knew there were no ill feelings between Maggie and my father but they had not been in contact since I was born and both had moved on in their lives. It must have been a very difficult period for Maggie but I was oblivious to her feelings. I had few considerations for the people around me at that point in my life.

I learnt more about my bloodline and my father. My father loved fighting, my grandfather had been a fighter, my uncles all fought. My uncle Patrick was one of the best fighting gypsies there was at the time. There was a huge amount of respect for the Doherty clan within the traveller community because of their reputation as hard men. They were bare-knuckle fighters. They fought the traveller way.

No Doherty would ever give best and the old man was the head of the clan. The old fella – my father Simey – was short but very stocky. He had the wide shoulders of a knuckle fighter – he was bred for combat. There was an air about him. He was quiet and brooding. He carried his name on his shoulders with pride but he was never arrogant. He knew his power. He was always well turned out. When I first met him he was wearing a cleanly laundered white shirt and I've rarely seen him without smart clothes on since. He was a grafter; he worked 24/7 if the work was there for him. Nowadays you'd call him a workaholic. He tarmacked and he dealt in metal and cars.

Doherty blood ran through my veins and that meant I came from true fighting stock. At around the age of 17 I graduated from the controlled environment of the boxing ring and took my first steps into the world of proper bare-knuckle fighting. I'd had fights before, mainly with country people, but they were reactionary fights on the spur of the moment. I didn't really count them as proper fights. Fighting travellers only hold stock in the fights they have with other travellers. They don't count fights in pubs with country men. Over the years I've had hundreds of scraps like that and it's as common to me as blowing my nose. If you fight a country man you don't boast about it because it's no big deal. A proper fight is one that's arranged between travellers. These are the fights that build reputations.

They say you never forget your first kiss, well for travellers of fighting stock, you never forget your first proper fight with a proper gypsy fighter. Going from boxing to bare-knuckle was a natural progression for me. I gave up boxing because I realised there was plenty of fighting to be had in my community. I was at a dance called Bellevue in Manchester. I was with Duck's Martin and at the dance there was a certain fellow who everyone was afraid of, the cock of the room. He was an English gypsy as opposed to an Irish traveller like me. There was no problem between the two communities but as a rule back then they didn't mix. I watched him and I could see he was pushing his way around. I was ten stone at the time and small. I had a feeling this man would bump into me just to push his weight around, so I stood there and watched him push other people and I brooded. I want a piece of him, I thought to myself. Halfway through the night I got my chance. He walked past me and he pushed me out the way to get on the dance floor.

'Don't push me, you sausage,' I sneered. I don't know where the word came from. But, I always thought sausages were full of useless pieces of meat that no one wanted so it just seemed like an apt insult.

'What did you call me?' the man shot back. He was at least five years older than me.

'I said you're a sausage,' I repeated.

People had started to look over at us. It was common for travellers to get into fights at Bellevue and they all knew where our exchange was leading.

'Let's sort this out properly,' I said to the man. He nodded. We picked an older man to show fair play and went outside into the car park and squared up to each other.

The adrenaline was racing through me when he threw his first punch. He was fast and it caught me on the cheek. I could take a punch. It didn't hurt and I instinctively hit him back. *Bang!* It was a clean hook straight on his jaw, and that was it. It was over. I didn't even realise at the time I had hit him that hard. He had gone straight down, crumpled like an empty sack. He was out cold on the floor.

I turned to Martin. 'What's wrong with him?' I asked.

'Paddy, you've killed the man,' Martin panicked.

'How could I?' I said. 'I only hit him once.'

The bouncers saw everything and came running out as the fair play man declared me the winner and my opponent's friends tried to revive him by slapping his face. The doormen grabbed me by the head and bundled me away.

We were banned from going back the following week but the week after that we got back in and I saw the same bloke again.

'I'm going to knock him out again with the same punch,' I told Martin, but when I went over to him and offered to fight him again he went white and refused. I told him if he had a problem I would cure it but he didn't want to know. My destiny was sealed in that one punch. That was it, my name started to get known from there beyond the confines of Heywood House and Cheatham Hill. It went out into the wider traveller community and I started to want the recognition that fighting attracted. I wanted to be the best. I went looking for fights.

There is no organisation to knuckle fighting; you don't have a governing body that arranges fights for you. You have to go and find them yourself. I could smell trouble; I was like a bee to honey. If I was in a pub or club and there was a fighter in there I would be able to sniff him out and I would want one crack, I would look at him and weigh him up. I'd look at him good and proper, like the way you look at a woman, up and down, I'd look at the width of his shoulders, the size of his hands and I'd initiate a fight. It was a very simple process.

'Come on, me and you, get your arse outside.' That's the way travellers were at that time. You'd have no argument and no reason other than competition. No one said no because it was all about keeping face. After that first fight I never turned a fight down, even if I knew I was going to lose I still believed I would win. I would still walk outside and battle even if I knew in my heart of hearts that I would get knocked out with two punches. I just couldn't turn down a fight. I'd get knocked down and I'd wake up and I'd do it again, that was just the way I was. I would get in fights every week. I went out looking for people with reputations.

A few months after I had met him for the first time, my father went away back down south to Bristol where he spent most of his time.

'Come and stay with me, son,' he said before he left. He wasn't a man to show emotion but I could tell it pained him to leave me. I knew he loved me in his way. For many years he had silently watched me from a distance as I grew. He wanted to be part of my life but kept away out of respect for my family. I was sad to see him go but I had become used to the people close to me drifting in and out of my life so I watched him go with a familiar numbness. I knew who he was and where I could find him.

Over the following months home life was difficult. I could feel the pull of my father and I could feel the pull of my mother. I was getting older, I was 17, and I was a man; I could make my own decisions. Travellers grow up quickly. I still longed to live a traveller life. A house just wasn't for me. I knew that I had a whole new family of travellers to stay with and the draw to leave home and go with them was getting stronger. The open road was beckoning me away from Maggie. I wanted to get back into a trailer.

A year earlier, in the autumn of 1975, I'd decided to leave Manchester and go and find my father. It was a rash decision and one I made after an argument with Maggie. I didn't even want her to know. I just wanted to disappear. But I didn't want to make the journey alone so I roped in my brother Martin.

'I'm going away,' I told him. 'I'm going to drive to Bristol to find my old man, do you want to come?'

We had pooled our money together to buy an old Avenger several months before. We hid it round the corner from the house and drove it without a licence. We were not old enough to drive at the time but that didn't stop us using it as a run-around on a daily basis. We never got stopped by the police. Martin was not too pleased about the idea of losing the car so he agreed to be my travelling companion. We didn't even pack. We got in the car and headed off down the M6 with hardly any money, no food and one of Davey Quinn's old coats. The heating in the car didn't work so we took it in turns to wear the coat.

After a few hours Martin began whinging. 'I'm hungry, I want tea.'

We stopped at a service station and bought some petrol and a Marathon bar. We used all the money we had and shared the chocolate for dinner. That night we slept in the car. I had one arm in the coat, Martin had one arm in the coat and we huddled for warmth in the middle. By the time the morning came we were tired, miserable and hungry and it dawned on me that we only had enough petrol to get us to Birmingham, certainly not to Bristol. We could carry on and hope a miracle happened and an opportunity to make money arose, or we could turn around and go back. The latter was the only sensible option and I turned round and headed back to Manchester defeated.

A year later the urge to leave home was stronger than ever. One day while Old Quinn was watching TV, I walked into the room and said simply: 'I'm going to stay with my father.'

Quinn looked at me with his wise eyes and nodded. He knew this day had been coming from the moment I found out about my dad.

'God send you luck and mind yourself on your way,' he replied.

This time proper arrangements were made. Davey Mary, a cousin of mine, was travelling to the south-west so he agreed to take me to Bristol in his Ford Escort van. There was a makeshift mattress in the back of it with blankets. It wasn't perfect but it was much more comfortable than being huddled in a coat with Martin, and I was close to Davey, so we had a good craic on the way. I packed my belongings and we set off. It was an adventure. I was heartless, I didn't stop to think how Maggie would feel and I never made plans to go back. I would go, find the old fella and see how the fancy took me; maybe I'd stay a few weeks, maybe I'd stay for ever. And with Davey accompanying me I knew I could always head back with him if it didn't work out.

My father was easy to find. In the days before mobile phones people talked and everyone knew everyone else's business. Travellers' lives were a network of camps and sites. You always knew someone wherever you went and they always knew someone who knew the person you wanted to find. You only had to stop at a site in a town and ask. It helped that the Dohertys were so well known. Most travellers had heard of my father. His fighting adventures figured in the stories that were told around the camp-fires at night.

When we pulled onto the site where he lived he came to greet us.

'It's good to see you Patrick, my son,' he smiled.

From the moment he met me, my father only ever called me Patrick, never Paddy. Even today I am Patrick to him. Initially it took some getting used to. I had a new name and a new family.

On the site my old fella, as I affectionately call him, took me to meet my sisters for the first time; Angela, Julie, Margaret, Mary and Jane, and his wife, Lizzie, who I call the Old Queen because that's who she is; my pa's queen. It was a tearful afternoon. The traveller code of secrecy meant that although the

Doherty clan knew I existed, I was never talked about. They had been waiting to meet me for many years.

The family lived on a camp in two big beautiful trailers. We call our trailers and our vehicles and belongings our 'turnout'. Your turnout shows the outside world what type of a person you are. It shows whether you are successful or not. The old man's turnout was impressive and marked him out as a wealthy man. As a traveller you could look at his turnout and see there was a lot of money there. His two trailers were Jubilees which were more or less the best make you could buy. He had one for him and the Old Queen and one for me and the other children. He also had a decent lorry and a car. Inside, the trailers were wall-to-wall fitted carpets and were bright and airy. They were decorated with cut glass, engraved fittings and the Old Queen proudly displayed her best china in glass-fronted cabinets.

That first night we ate together and then I slept in Davey's van. The next day Davey and I messed around all day on the site and went for a drive around the local area.

'I'm going back to Manchester, Paddy,' he said, as we were driving through the countryside.

The reality of the situation hit me. Davey was my one link to my family in Manchester. When he left the door for me to return would close. Manchester and Bristol were a long way apart in those days and the chances of me getting back easily were slim if things didn't work out for me with my dad.

'Please don't go, Davey,' I said. I loved having him there and we were having so much fun. The drive to the south-west and the two days we had spent there had been like a holiday.

But Davey had work to do back up north. He had done his duty and delivered me to my father and it was time for him to return home. When he went I went to pieces. The enormity of what I was doing hit me. I had been so eager to go off and join my father I didn't even think about what I was leaving behind. I was there with strangers I didn't really know and my exit route out had closed. I did what I used to do when I was truanting from school and wandered off in to the country alone, sitting for hours crying my heart out. I felt like a little kid again. I stayed out for five hours just sitting and thinking. Then I pulled myself together and went back to my father's camp. When I got there he ran out of the trailer and hugged me.

'Where have you been, Patrick?' he asked. I could see he was visibly upset. 'I thought you had left me. Never go again without telling me where you are going. I thought you'd gone back to Manchester, my heart was broken.'

I was stunned. The old fella really did love me and it tore at his heart to think that after so many years apart I had moved on again.

'If you ever want to leave me, just tell me,' he said. 'But never disappear without letting me know.' I realised then just how much he cared for me.

Over the following weeks I got to know my new family. I got close to my uncle Johnny. He was a man I really looked up to and admired. I wanted to be like him and he explained about the code that Doherty men live by.

'You never give best Patrick,' he told me. 'If you have to die, then die, but never tell another man he has bested you, never give in.'

The reality of what it meant to be a Doherty and what would be expected of me began to sink in. My father's name meant something. During my time in Bristol I saw him in action fighting a few times and he took no prisoners. When he fought he wanted to hurt severely. He was a different kind of fighter to me. Once I had beaten an opponent I left him. I knew when a man had had enough. But the old man wouldn't stop, he'd only stop when he'd had enough. Dad would growl, 'You've had enough when I tell you you've had enough.'

I formed a close bond with my sister Angela. She was younger than me but the eldest child in the family and she worshipped me. The Old Queen was very good to me and accepted me as one of the family without reservation. She was a kind woman and very religious. I was too ignorant at the time to notice but it must have been hard on her when all of a sudden I came out of nowhere to live with her and her family.

I went out to work with my father every day. We became close and got to know about each other and each other's lives. I had no friends in Bristol, sometimes cousins would come and visit me but they always left after a couple of days, but it didn't matter. I didn't miss anything about Manchester and my life in the north. I felt I was where I belonged, back in a trailer on a site with travelling people. I had the freedom I was missing for so many years and freedom was everything to me. As time went on I travelled with the old man further afield to find work.

You would find out about profitable places to stay through word of mouth. If a traveller stayed in a place where there was work, he would always tell other travellers he met. Back then everyone trusted each other as no one would ever dream of lying. It was a big deal to move, you would have to uproot everything, especially if you had a family, so you had to be able to trust each other and trust the information other travellers gave you. The best places for work were Scotland and Wales where there were lots of villages out in the middle of nowhere. They were the kind of places where people still needed things done or had scrap metal to get rid of.

Travellers didn't have specific villages or streets they worked. It was every man for his self. If you went to an area and there was already a traveller working it, you'd make friends with him. You'd go to the pub with him and you'd get to know each other. There was no such thing as business rivals, only friends.

In the end I stayed with my dad in Bristol for a year. It was longer than I've stayed in a lot of places since. While I was there he bought me my first van and I was eager to get out on my own in it and start earning a living for myself.

Despite my father's reputation I never fought in front of him at that time. I was never a bully and I only went looking for fights with other fighting men. Later in life, as my reputation grew, violence came looking for me but in Bristol I was like a fish out of water. I was just settling in so fighting wasn't on my mind. I could never turn down an opportunity though. One day, a fighting friend of my father's arrived on site and heard about my reputation. He asked my father if he could take me to a big fight in London with him that he was attending. His name was Dave and he was a true gentleman. I'd seen plenty of fights before but I'd never been to the capital to witness one of the big fights, the type that became folklore. My father agreed to let me go and all the way there Dave told me about the fights he had seen.

'There's buckets of blood and snot and the fighters will take each other to the brink of death, but the next day they'll have a pint with each other and have a laugh about it all,' he explained.

The more I heard, the more I wanted a go myself. At these big fights, other fights often broke out or were arranged.

When we reached the site of the fight, on wasteland in Walthamstow, east London, there were hundreds of travellers there. The atmosphere was electric and people had travelled from all over the country. I can't remember who the men were but I remember the blood. Dave wasn't exaggerating. Blow after blow was exchanged until the concrete underneath the men was smeared with red.

Many of the travellers went to a pub nearby afterwards. After the morning's entertainment there was raw aggression in the air. Everyone, including me, was fired up.

A man approached me.

'So this is the famous Paddy Ward is it?' he asked. I could tell by the mocking tone in his voice that he didn't want a friendly chat. 'You're smaller than I imagined,' he sneered.

It was the first time I had been picked out by my reputation outside of the north-west. This man knew who I was. But I wasn't flattered, far from it. He was calling me Ward to goad me and he was making fun of my height.

'You're a small wee thing, aren't you?' he laughed patronisingly.

'Leave the kid alone and fuck off,' said Dave.

But I didn't need anyone to protect me. Sure this man was older and bigger than me but I knew I could take him.

'Let me fight him Dave,' I begged. I was like a terrier straining at the leash. Dave looked at me and he could see how eager I was. He could also see the belief in my eyes, perhaps he recognised it from himself.

'Go on then,' he nodded.

We went outside and I went for the man. I was small and wiry but I packed a punch and it was a good fight for about four minutes then it came my way. I cut him across the bridge of the nose and dropped him with a perfect uppercut. Dave put me on his shoulders and started dancing. He took me back to my old man the next day.

'Simey, he's good,' he told the old fella. 'He's as good as you were in your day.'

They were lovely days, getting to know my family but my old man worked me hard. I'd do the tar all day, shovelling and wheeling and then he'd drop me off somewhere and tell me to run home to get fit. I didn't realise it then but he was training me up.

One day, almost on impulse, I decided it was time to move on.

'I'm going back up north,' I told the old man. I had done the same to Davey Quinn a year before and my father had the same look in his eye old Quinn had. He knew this day would come.

'Be lucky, Patrick,' he said to me.

Our roots were firmly entwined by then. When I arrived I had been a Ward. I was leaving a Doherty: a fighting man.

6

All's Fair in Love and War

'I'm looking for Paddy Ward, which one of you is he?'

I'd never seen the man before in my life but I could tell by the tone of his voice what he wanted. He was a giant, around six foot with a broad chest and shoulder muscles straining under his T-shirt. He was standing with several other men and I recognised a few of them. I'd had trouble with them in another pub earlier in the day. We'd got into an argument over something or another and they'd left before it came to violence.

I was back in Manchester in a pub with my father and uncles who had come to visit. I was 18 and we were having a craic. It felt good to be with the Doherty men. I was part of a family. The old man was drinking a pint, I was on orange juice. I never drank back then. I didn't like the taste of alcohol and I wanted a clear head because increasingly when I went out, I got into fights.

I looked the man who had asked after me up and down. It seemed today was going to be no exception.

I'd been Paddy Ward all my life and that was still how most people referred to me. But I had discovered I was a Doherty and whenever I heard myself referred to as Ward, I felt the mistake needed to be redressed. I wasn't ashamed of the mixed names. The Wards and the McDonaghs are good people and I was proud to be part of them, but I was my father's son and traveller lore dictated that I should take his name.

'I'm Paddy Doherty,' I snarled at the man. 'What's it to you?'

It was the first time I'd used the name in public and in front of my father and it felt good. It felt right coming out of my mouth. I caught the old man looking at me with pride. I wanted him to see how proud I was of my name. There was a lot resting on my shoulders as the oldest Doherty son. I wanted to impress and I wanted to be accepted.

The man smiled but there was no humour in his face.

'Whatever your name is, boy, we have business.' He nodded his head towards the toilets. He wasn't inviting me there for a cosy chat.

His friends were jostling to get at me too. With their giant friend backing them up they had suddenly become brave.

Since my first traveller fight, I'd developed a reputation. The more fights I'd won, the more people knew my name. Word had begun to spread that I was turning out to be a decent fighter and was fast becoming the man to beat. I'd won every fight I had taken part in up to that point. You are as good as the best man you beat and I had beaten some good men. Fighting had become my preoccupation. I was good at it. Very good. I would look out for fighting men. In pubs and clubs and dances I could spot them a mile off. It was like being part of a secret fraternity; like the Masons. Usually I'd get lucky and it would be obvious who the man to beat was in any given venue. He'd make himself known either by the way he held himself or by using the traveller sign of placing a glass upside down on the table in front of him. Anyone who does that in a pub is giving the signal that he thinks he's the top man in the place. He is saying 'I'm the only one who can turn this glass back up the right way.' He's asserting his authority over every other man in the place. It's a sign to other fighters, a challenge. It is arrogant and it can be danger-ous. If you turn your glass upside down in a travellers' pub, you better have the ammunition to back up your claim. It's not something I'd ever do. It's cocky.

If it wasn't immediately obvious who the man to beat was, I'd ask around. Often it would be one of the doormen. Increasingly I'd find out who the man who ran the doormen was. There is always someone above them who they look up to and respect. Why beat the monkey when you can have a crack at the organ grinder?

That day, in the pub with my father, I hadn't had to go look-ing: trouble found me.

'I'll fight one of you,' I addressed the group of men. 'The winner walks out the pub unharmed and it's forgotten.'

That was the code travellers lived by. After a fair fight there were no repercussions. An argument was finished the moment a man was beat.

The big chap nodded. It was obvious he was the one I was going to have to fight. Size never bothered me though. I learnt early on in my fighting career that just because an opponent was big, didn't mean he could fight. Some of the best fighters with the hardest punches were small wiry men. When I boxed I had always picked the biggest opponents to spar with and I had no problem fighting men a foot taller than me. I followed the hulk into the men's toilet, thinking to myself that he would regret his choice of venue.

There are different types of fighters. There are those who prefer to fight outside in open space and there are pub fighters – men who like to slug it out surrounded by glasses and bottles and furniture. These men are dangerous because they don't play by the rules. They use whatever is at hand as a weapon. They care little about cutting and slashing an opponent with broken glass or battering him with a barstool. I preferred to fight fair, in the open; most travellers did, but I had no problem fighting indoors if I had to. The man I was following into the toilet was a pub fighter but I could tell he was an inexperienced one. If he knew anything about fighting he would have chosen to stay in the bar. For a big man there was no advantage at all to fighting in the confined space of a toilet but plenty of pitfalls. I pointed one out to him the minute the door closed behind us and one of the doormen from the pub stood across it to stop any interference. As he turned and swung at me, I dodged his fist, grabbed the side of his head and smashed it into the ceramic tiles on the wall. He staggered back dazed. Only one of us would be leaving the room on our feet.

The close quarters meant we were right up in each other's faces, which was fine by me. I loved getting in close. The big chap however was struggling. His long arms were useless without space to extend the swing of his punches and he had no room to use his weight advantage. *Crack!* I caught him with a beautiful hook straight to his temple. I followed it up with an

Me as a baby.
A happy little soul.

Me, aged ten.

Daddy and Mummy Ward.

My real father Simey, as a young man.

(L-R) Winnie & her husband Old Christie Joyce and Old Davey Quinn & his sister Cathleen.

My days at Ardwick Boys Club were the making of me.

My beautiful Roseanne and me on our wedding day. Look at that hair!

Getting my first born,
my Par, baptised.

Me and Patrick outside
the caravan.

A young buck training hard.

A sunny day
with the family.

All dressed up for
Confirmation day!

My sons Simey (left) and Johnny (below) following in their daddy's footsteps.

uppercut that rocked his head back and sent a gob of bloody spit spraying over his shoulder. He was going down, and as he did he grabbed me in a bear hug to try and contain any more punches, but I could feel his knees start to weaken. I tried to wriggle out but he was holding on for dear life and I only managed to turn round so my back was to him and his arms were clasped together around my waist. I butted back with my head trying to get him in the face and kicked back with my foot into his kneecap. I caught him square on the joint and heard the cartilage in his knee crunch as his leg gave way. We both went down and as we did I managed to get one hand free. As I reached round and grabbed the back of his head he reached down and grabbed my nuts. He squeezed so hard I thought they were going to pop. The pain was sickening but I knew I had a chance to finish the fight. We were both on our knees, our faces level with a white porcelain wash basin. I rammed his face into it with my free hand. His nose split. I smashed his face against the sink again and widened the cut. I don't know how many times I cracked his face against the basin in the end but a tooth came out and his nose and mouth had mashed into one ugly wound by the time I finished. With each blow I felt his grip on my bollocks loosen until he let go completely and slumped backwards on the cold floor semi-conscious. He was breathing heavily and the blood was gurgling in his throat. I turned him over to make sure he didn't choke and got unsteadily to my feet.

The old man told me later that when I walked out the door he got a glimpse of the inside of the toilet. The floor was covered in blood. It looked like a scene from a horror movie. No one bothered us in the pub again. We were given a wide berth. A little while later the group of men walked past with their friend. He'd been cleaned up and looked like he needed stitches. His puffy eyes were almost swollen shut. He nodded to me as he limped past.

'If I can't have kids, I'll come looking for you,' I half-joked. The ache in my groin was still eye-watering.

Thankfully, not every trip out resulted in a fight. I wasn't always looking for trouble, usually it just found me.

I found a lot more than I bargained for in a dance called the Carousel in Manchester. Her name was Roseanne and from the minute I laid eyes on her I knew I had to make her mine. It was like a scene from a movie. I saw her in slow motion. I was with my brother Martin and she was with her sister Theresa, who Martin was dating. Roseanne was walking towards us up an alleyway by the side of the club. She was wearing a flowing tunic and jeans and the neon lights of the high street behind her outlined her silhouette. The wind took her long dark hair and blew it back from her face, which was a thing of beauty. It was young and pure. I stood there like a cartoon character, my jaw slack. I'd had a few girlfriends but nothing serious. The minute I saw Roseanne I knew I fancied her more than any woman I'd ever met. My heart raced a million times faster than it ever had.

I looked over at Martin.

'She's a good-looking young woman,' I sighed.

'I'll introduce you,' he offered.

When he did Roseanne didn't give me the time of day. She was only 16 and she was a Gallagher. They were a well-to-do Irish family. I was a Doherty; I came from a family of fighters. Doherty men were known for their love of violence and uncompromising nature. But like all Dohertys, I fight hard and love strong. I'm a traveller and those are the two things that come most natural to us. And as soon as I saw Roseanne I wanted to give my love to her. She was just a girl; she was sweet and innocent. I was a rough piece of coal and she was a diamond. That night I tried not to show her how struck I was with her. I compensated for nervousness with arrogance and cockiness. We had a dance and I told her I'd like to see her again.

'Maybe,' she shrugged.

Luck was on my side, however. Martin got serious with Theresa and traveller custom meant that Theresa could not be on her own with him. Single girls always have to be chaperoned by friends or family members. Travellers are very moral and decent people. We don't allow our daughters to be alone with men. Theresa's chaperone was Roseanne but Roseanne complained that she was bored when she accompanied them and had no one to talk to.

'I'll bring my brother Paddy along then,' suggested Martin. In that one sentence he did me the biggest favour of my life.

Over the following weeks I got to know Roseanne and she got to know me. Despite the difference in our family backgrounds, she started to thaw. Martin would walk with Theresa and I would walk with Roseanne. That's what we did in those days – we'd just walk together, or go to a dance or to the cinema.

Eventually Martin asked Theresa to marry him. He was brave doing it because he had to ask permission from her father, Paddy Gallagher, who was very old-fashioned and very strict.

Even though they were engaged to be married, Theresa still had to be accompanied when she was with Martin so my time with Roseanne and the bride and groom-to-be continued. Maybe it was because romance was in the air but Roseanne and I got closer. We walked arm in arm.

I knew what I wanted and what I wanted was her. But while I thought nothing of facing up to the biggest, hardest bloke in the place, my legs turned to jelly whenever I thought of asking Roseanne if she would go with me. We didn't call it going out. It meant becoming boyfriend and girlfriend.

We were with Martin and Theresa on one of our walks, following a few paces behind them. I wasn't myself – usually when we went out together, the conversation between us would just flow, but tonight I was going to ask her to go with me, but I just couldn't pluck up the courage.

It didn't help that she looked so beautiful that night, more beautiful than I had ever seen her. She got more beautiful by the day.

Roseanne made a comment about something or other and I hardly heard her – I was too wrapped up in choosing my moment, saying the right words, wanting to ask her but desperately worried that she might say no. And what would happen then?

'Paddy?' She stopped walking and put her hand on my arm. 'Is something wrong? Is it something with your family?'

I looked into her face, into those beautiful eyes. Her forehead was wrinkled in concern.

'It's just that—'

I couldn't say it, I couldn't find the words.

'What is it, Paddy?'

I looked down at my feet. This was my moment. I gathered up every single ounce of courage that I had and said, 'It's just that... Roseanne Gallagher,' I looked up, into her face and said quietly, 'will you go with me?'

Her expression changed from worry into what looked like part-relief, part-happiness. 'Yes, of course, I will, Paddy Doherty. I've been waiting for you to ask me that.'

They were the sweetest words I'd ever heard.

For about three or four months Roseanne would come and see me in the daytime and make sure she was home again by 5 p.m. for when her father came back from work. As we fell deeper for each other, we stayed together later and later into the evening. We didn't do anything improper. She was a clean-living girl with a lot of respect for herself and her family and I respected her too. We talked about everything and anything; the little day-to-day things that people in love talk about and big things too. I told her about my family and my mixed-up childhood. I talked about fighting but she never liked to hear about such things. She was a peaceful girl. We began to fall in love and we talked about getting married. My heart sang when she said she would like to marry me. I knew Roseanne was my future. Time didn't seem to matter when I was with her. What seemed like minutes were actually hours.

One afternoon I took her to meet my family. We went to Aunt Mary's; Davey Quinn's sister. Then I took her to see my father, who was in town, and we sat up all night talking. Roseanne got back in the early hours of the morning and I knew I was in trouble. We'd done nothing wrong and had been with my family, but in the eyes of her father, I had committed a sin. Even though nothing had happened between us, I'd kept his daughter out all night, which was a big scandal and brought shame on their family's name.

The next day Roseanne and I met up again. As soon as I saw her face I knew something was wrong, and to be honest, I had been expecting it. It was wrong of me to keep Roseanne out all night – it isn't what travellers do when they're courting and I knew that I was going to have to answer to her father.

'Was he mad?' I asked gently.

Roseanne nodded. She looked as if she hadn't got any sleep, and her eyes looked puffy, as if she had been crying. 'He's going to want to see you, Paddy. He's furious with both of us.'

That was it then. I had to face up to the man. 'I'll walk you home,' I said, apprehension twisting my stomach into knots.

As we were walking back to her house, I saw her father Paddy coming along the road towards us. He looked livid. I hadn't met him at this point and I assumed he was going to batter me. There wasn't a thing I could do about it, I couldn't even hit him back because he was an older man and travellers did not attack older people. It was forbidden, we showed respect to older people.

'Don't run,' he said to me.

'I'm not running,' I said.

He ordered Roseanne to go home, fetch her mother and meet us in the pub across the street, which he ushered me into.

A few minutes later Roseanne came in with her mum. She looked ashen. No one knew what Paddy Gallagher was going to do. I thought he'd probably steady his nerves with a whisky and then stick a bottle in my neck.

'What do you want to drink?' he growled to me.

'I'll have a Coke, please,' I replied.

'You'll have a what?' he questioned.

'A Coke,' I answered.

Paddy straightened up to his full height. 'I won't ask you again, what do you want to drink?' he said.

'All right, I'll have orange,' I shrugged. I didn't have a clue why he couldn't understand my order.

'Listen, son,' he said, poking his finger at my chest, 'if you are man enough to run away with my daughter, you'll be man enough to take a man's drink out of me.'

They were powerful words and when he said them I looked to Roseanne.

'Don't even look at me,' she hissed.

I turned back to her father. 'I'll have half a Guinness then please,' I said.

He looked me in the eye. 'No man drinks a half. A man drinks a pint,' he said and ordered me a pint.

It was not the right time to tell him I didn't drink, so when the glass came I put it to my lips and pretended to drink it. I felt like a condemned man having his last request.

Paddy took a long gulp of his pint and breathed in deeply.

'So, your brother Martin is marrying my Theresa?' It was a rhetorical question. I nodded.

And then he dropped a bombshell.

'I'll see the priest and get you married the same day, then,' he said.

If I'd had a mouthful of beer at the time I would have spat it out in shock. But the reasoning made sense. Roseanne and I had discussed marriage. We were going together and the next step to that in those days was marriage. Although I hadn't officially asked Paddy, I had kept his daughter out all night and that meant I had to commit to her, which I was more than happy to do.

So that was it. That was how I ended up betrothed to the woman of my dreams. Roseanne was just 16 and I was 18.

I said thank you very much to Paddy.

'You'd better go and tell Maggie and Davey Quinn,' he advised. He could barely hide his contempt. I was weightless when I walked out the pub. All my cockiness came flooding back and I winked at Roseanne as I left.

Back in Maggie's house where I was living at the time the news that her eldest son was getting married was met with as much enthusiasm as Paddy had shown.

I told my mother the story of how I'd accidentally kept Roseanne out. 'God forgive you,' she said and gave me a slap. Rough discipline, perhaps, but I was under her roof and by keeping Roseanne out until the early hours, I had damaged her reputation, which means everything to a traveller woman. And perhaps Maggie was remembering what had happened to her, how she had to give me up because I was born out of wedlock.

Eventually she had met Davey Quinn, and things had turned out all right for her, but life had been hard, and it must have been a shock for her. She must have wondered whether history was repeating itself.

I tried to plead with her that I did nothing wrong and that it was just the one time, but she was disgusted with me. I didn't care. I wanted to marry Roseanne more than anything in the world.

Paddy's attitude softened to me over the years. He was a lovely man; he was reasonable and fair and gave me a chance and the benefit of the doubt. I hope I didn't disappoint him and with my hand on my heart I can say that I have always loved his daughter above everything else.

I became his favourite son-in-law. In later life he lost both his legs to gangrene. I'll always remember how one day when we were both much older we were in a pub in London together. I got him a whisky and water and I had a bottle of lager for myself and as we sat supping he turned to me and said: 'You know Paddy son, I want to tell you, I've got a lot of son-in-laws but I wouldn't give the dirt out of your nail for every one of them.'

I was an arse. I pretended not to hear him. I had to get him to say it twice.

'You heard me,' he smiled. 'I love you very much. I know you mind my Roseanne. Will you always mind her?'

'Of course I will,' I promised, 'all my life.'

7

My Gypsy Wedding

A lot has been said about gypsy weddings. I've been part of the show that made them famous, so I have to take some responsibility. What I can say is that the big extravagant ceremonies you see on the television do happen, but not every gypsy has a big fat wedding. We are like any other people. Some have big weddings and like to show off; others have small affairs.

For travellers it is customary for the father of the bride to pay for everything. And that can be expensive. Once the father has agreed to give his daughter away, the groom can dictate what type of wedding he wants down to the last detail and usually with a bit of pressure from his bride. He can request an open bar, a stag weekend with ten of his mates and he can name the venue. Travellers don't talk about money. We think it's rude for people to ask the cost of things so for that reason you will never discover how much a really big wedding costs. However, you don't have to be a wedding planner to work out that a big wedding with all the trappings isn't cheap. You are looking at tens of thousands of pounds. So if you are a traveller with a lot of daughters you're screwed!

My wedding to Roseanne was not a big affair. We had no fairytale carriage or ten-stone wedding dress. It was hastily arranged and tacked on to the end of my brother's wedding. At the time I had no savings and Paddy had already spent his money on Theresa's wedding. At first I had a chip on my shoulder. I wanted the best for my bride like any groom would, but our wedding was going to be cobbled together. We had only been going steady for four months and had no time to arrange anything or put some money aside for it. But as the day got nearer I began to care less and less. The only thing that mattered to me was that I was marrying the girl of my dreams. The details were irrelevant.

Roseanne managed to borrow a dress from a friend. It only cost a few pounds and it was plain compared to the dresses girls wear today. There were no crystals sewn into it. It was white and fitted. She took it in herself and added a few adjustments to make it her own. It didn't matter that it wasn't tailor-made. What mattered was the person inside it and no matter what Roseanne wore, she always looked beautiful.

While Roseanne managed to sort out her dress, I was having no success with a ring. I didn't care about having one myself but what I did care about was having one to put on my bride's finger at the altar. I had no money to buy one. I couldn't borrow one and I didn't feel comfortable about trying to find a second-hand one. I'm not overly superstitious but I wanted my Roseanne to be able to wear a ring that hadn't been worn by someone else. Eventually my uncle Johnny came to the rescue.

About a week before the wedding he came to see me and pulled two brand-new gold bands out of his pocket. They were not in boxes but there wasn't a mark on them.

'Do you want them for your wedding?' he asked.

I had no money at the time.

'I can't afford them,' I told him.

'Don't worry about that Paddy, you can have them,' he offered.

I wasn't about to look a gift horse in the mouth and gratefully accepted them. I turned them over in my hand, weighing them up. They were genuine gold and heavy. I couldn't believe my luck.

'Thank you so much, Uncle,' I said.

'Don't mention it, my nephew,' he smiled and walked off down the path.

As an after-thought I called after him, 'Where did you get them?'

He turned. 'I robbed them from the market,' he smiled.

I decided it was best to keep that fact quiet. I felt the guilt weigh me down when the day came to say my vows, but I had no choice. I'd rather put a stolen ring on my bride's finger than suffer the shame of having no ring at all. I didn't dare tell Roseanne where her wedding ring came from for many years. When I did finally confess she made sure I bought her a legitimate one.

The wedding day was a dramatic roller coaster. I married my Roseanne on 20 August 1977. I was 18, she had just turned 17; still a child. When she walked down the aisle with her daddy she was the most beautiful thing I had ever seen.

It hadn't been long since I had found out my true heritage and many of the guests still thought of me as a Ward. Many of them knew nothing about my real father so when the priest began to recite the vows and used my new name there was an audible gasp.

'Do you, Patrick Douglas Doherty...' he began.

I held my head up high and enjoyed the moment. I was arrogant and I still had a chip on my shoulder about being lied to for so long. That was my way of getting back at all the people who hid my past from me. It must have hurt some people to hear that name in open church but it was who I was and I was not about to lie in the house of God.

My father wasn't at the ceremony. I wish he had been there to hear it but it would have caused too many problems. My sister Angela was in church instead to represent the Doherty side of my family and he came later in the day. It was big news in the traveller community. The Doherty family was well known and my addition to it was talked about across the country.

Roseanne and I stood at the altar with Martin and Theresa. They were the golden couple. Martin had a new suit on and Theresa had a lovely dress. I wore a suit that didn't fit and Roseanne had her borrowed dress on. We piggybacked on the back of some else's big day. We didn't even have a cake and I was too proud to beg for some of Martin's so I went without. But in the moment that we said our vows and she gave herself to me, money didn't matter a thing to me; I was the richest man in the world.

The reception was a joint affair too. There was a buffet but I didn't eat. I didn't really care. What mattered to me was that I put a ring on Roseanne's finger. She was mine then. I had my wife.

For her part Roseanne spent most of the day in tears. She was dazed by it all. Just a few months before she was a daddy's girl without a care in the world. Suddenly she had been thrown into my world; the rough world of the Dohertys with all its secrets. I was a fighter with a reputation for trouble and she was as pure as the driven snow.

When my father arrived for the reception you could have heard a pin drop. There had been whispers all day about whether he would have shown up, and I'm sure a few bets placed too! Even so people were shocked that he had come. He was a respectful man and he waited until Maggie and Davey Quinn had left before he entered the room. He didn't care what everyone else thought. It was the first time Simey had shown his face to the Wards and the McDonaghs and some reasoned that he would stay away in order to keep the peace. I knew him better. He was scared of no man and I was his first-born son. He wasn't losing me again and he wanted to be part of my life.

Everyone's attention was drawn towards the short, stocky figure that just came through the door. I stood up, took my beautiful bride by the hand, and walked towards him.

'Son,' my father said, and grasped my arm, 'congratulations.'

He turned to Roseanne. 'Welcome to the family, my love,' he said, and kissed her on the cheek. I glanced round. People were turning back to each other.

In the afternoon I went outside for some air and Angela followed me out. She was my little sister and there was a close bond between us. She was a beautiful girl and she told me how pleased she was for both me and Roseanne. Like all women at weddings she was emotional and she hugged me and gave me a kiss. As she did my new brother-in-law, Paddy, walked past. He shot me a look of hatred and as Angela pulled away from me and walked back in to the venue he walked over to me and without a word of explanation hit me square in the face. He busted my lip.

'What the fuck was that for?' I said.

'You're going to die, you bastard,' he said. 'What kind of a man goes with another woman on his wedding day? How dare you! My sister is in there and it's her wedding day.'

'You fucking idiot,' I answered. 'That was *my* sister.'

I wanted to smash him in the face but I couldn't bring myself to beat my new wife's brother on her wedding day.

The realisation of what he'd done sunk in. Paddy went white.

'I'm so sorry Paddy,' he stuttered. 'I didn't realise.' He offered me his hand to shake and he bought me a drink.

Inside the venue Roseanne looked at my lip in shock. 'What happened to your mouth?' she asked.

'Your stupid brother just hit me,' I told her.

He is dead now, God rest him, and we laughed about it years later. It was one of the only times in my life when someone hit me and I walked away.

At the end of the night my bride and I had no hotel or house to go to. My father took me aside and said: 'Son, you are sleeping with me tonight.' He wanted to prove a point; that I belonged to him. So on our wedding night I slept next to my father in his new estate car and she slept with my aunt. Initially we moved in with my uncle Paddy and aunt Bridgie. They were very hospitable but still it was awkward. We were there sharing a trailer and I was a newly married man. I worked hard and saved my money. The site we lived on was in Leigh, near Manchester, off the East Lancs Road and next to a coal mine. There was a river running across a field at the bottom of it. My father wanted to give me money to make a start and buy my own trailer but I refused. He was a very proud man and he wanted to start off his son but I was equally as proud and I wanted to do things myself to prove that I could look after my woman.

I got married that day with no house to go to and nothing in my name. On my wedding night I lay awake listening to my old man snoring and I thought to myself, bollocks to this, I really better start saving.

8

My Woman

Being married gave me a new perspective on life. I was 18 and in the eyes of the law I was a man, but I soon discovered that being a real man had nothing to do with age, it was about being selfless. Until then, I had never had responsibility for anyone other than myself. Suddenly the realisation hit me that life was no longer just about me; I had a wife to support.

Country people might think it is old-fashioned and sexist, but traveller men are expected to provide for their wives. It's what marriage is about. It is a mutual agreement. We are the providers and in return our women look after us. They cook and clean and they enjoy doing it. When I got married it was very rare for a traveller's wife to go out and work. Nowadays some do but the majority still stay at home and look after their families. It's the man's responsibility to earn the money and if he doesn't, he's not a proper man. I had to make sure Roseanne had a place to live and food to cook. In the past I had been able to come and go as I chose. There was always somewhere for me to stay in any part of the country, thanks to my extended family. There were Wards, McDonaghs and Dohertys everywhere. I rarely had to pay for my lodgings or the food on my plate. I took it all for granted. I was selfish.

But in the days and weeks after my wedding all that changed. I had a wife and she needed a home. So for the first few months of our married life, while we lived with Paddy and Bridgie, I worked all the hours I could laying tarmac with Davey Quinn to make enough money to buy a trailer. I would go out at dawn and work until my hands were covered in blisters. I had renewed purpose. The fear of not being able to provide for my new wife spurred me on. When I was hawking on the doorstep I was extra nice to the country people to try and pick up more trade.

My Roseanne had trouble adjusting to our new life. She wanted to go home. She felt lost and alone. Travellers are blunt people. If you are not used to their ways they can come across as hard and Bridgie was constantly telling Roseanne to take the other travellers on the site with a pinch of salt and not to take their gruff comments to heart. Roseanne explained later that if it wasn't for Bridgie helping her and showing her trailer life, she would have insisted we move into a house.

In her home Roseanne had been the cleaner and she helped Bridgie around the trailer. One morning, I told her to try and make an effort with the cooking as that was what she would be expected to do. She set fire to the frying pan and almost burned the trailer down.

Every day I put aside the pounds I'd earned and soon I had a small bundle of notes. It was the first time I'd saved money properly and it felt good to know that I was worth something. Eventually I scrimped together enough money to buy our first trailer. It was second-hand and it cost £200. It was a small two-berth caravan. It wasn't anything to look at. It was old and draughty, but it was mine.

I hooked it up to my van and drove it to show Roseanne. She looked it over without a word. She didn't have to say anything. I knew it wasn't what she was used to; she had lived in a house before she married me so she would have trouble adjusting. But I vowed it was just the start. Before long we would have a turnout to make our parents proud. In my heart of hearts I believed it.

Summer was almost over and it got colder and colder in that old caravan. We spent our nights huddled under sheets listening to the rain on the roof and trying to block the leaking holes. If it was raining and the wind was blowing in a particular direction, the water would come in by the bed and we'd wake in the morning wrapped in wet blankets.

We always cooked in the trailer and we had a fire outside. We had a little baby frying pan because there was just the two of us. We'd hardly watch telly because we just talked. We were just getting to know each other. I wasn't bad-looking and to me Roseanne was the most beautiful woman I had ever seen in my life. Her teeth were white, her skin was pink, her hair was jet black (I thought it was natural, it took me a year to realise it was dyed. I still don't know what her natural colour is).

When we were first married we didn't go out for meals. We didn't believe in going to restaurants. If you were out and very drunk you would maybe go to a Chinese or Indian and sit in but I never drank at that time so I never went.

I didn't mind the wet and the cold, I loved being in a trailer. I loved the sound of the world outside, unhindered by brick walls. The wind sang to us and rocked us to sleep. For Roseanne however, they were cruel living conditions. She was so young and the culture shock of moving away from the security of her ma and pa to living with me weighed heavy on her.

But we loved each other and despite everything we had many laughs. We made plans for the future. We both wanted children, the more the better. We both came from big families and wanted a big family for ourselves. We didn't have very much money and what I did earn, I saved. I didn't want my Roseanne to be in that small trailer for long and if we were to have children, we'd need bigger accommodation.

Even with no money for nice things, Roseanne always managed to look beautiful. She always looked different and begged and borrowed outfits from friends and relatives. She was never shy about telling me what she expected of a husband. From the day I married her she made it clear that she expected me to provide a decent living for her and our family. She was always telling me to go out and work and earn. She made me save hard. And I never looked back. She made me more responsible and she made me look ahead, which I had never done before. She was like an anchor; she made me put down roots. In all honesty I think I'd be dead now if it wasn't for her. I really believe that. Before I met her I really didn't care about myself or my life, but she cared for me.

Roseanne never complained even though I knew her heart was broken because she'd left her parents and many times in those early months she wanted her mummy and daddy back.

Even so, those days were the best of our lives. Looking back, considering what happened after, I realise now that back then we didn't have a care in the world.

My old way of life went out the window and I fell into a lifestyle that I wasn't used to, one of responsibility. Some days I hankered after my past but once I was married there was no turning back. If I didn't provide for my wife I would have failed. The shame would be so disgraceful I wouldn't be able to show my face to the world. It would be worse than getting divorced and that's one thing you never hear of a traveller doing.

While I was settling into the domestic bliss of married life, the community I had grown up in was alive with gossip about the revelation at the altar during my wedding that I was a Doherty and not a Ward.

It was a big scandal and it began to be used against me by men looking for trouble. People would call me Paddy Ward just to rile me because Paddy Ward was no longer my name. 'I'm Paddy Doherty,' I would tell them through gritted teeth. It was like calling me a bastard. I would always react and would go straight into fight mode. I never needed an excuse. I might have discovered responsibility when it came to being a husband and a provider, but fighting wasn't wrong in my culture. Fighting wasn't irresponsible behaviour. It was a way of dealing with issues and sorting out differences. It was practically a form of communication. You didn't bother arguing, you punched to get your point across.

A few months after we had moved into our first trailer Roseanne got her first taste of traveller injustice. When I met her she was innocent to the ways of the outside world and had been sheltered to the prejudice that travellers faced. She wasn't stupid. She knew what country people thought of travellers but she had never been at the sharp end of it. Her father did a good job keeping her safe and happy. Out on the road with me, she was as exposed and vulnerable to the unfairness of country life as every other travelling gypsy.

We were staying on a plot of land outside Manchester with several other families. We had put our trailers on a site that had been recommended by other travellers as a safe place to stop over for a couple of nights. We were only staying for a day or so before moving on to somewhere more permanent. The bailiffs came early in the morning like they always did. We were still asleep when they battered on the door. The frame of the old caravan buckled under their heavy hands.

'Get off this land, you scum,' they yelled.

They were waving a piece of paper around. It didn't matter what it said and whether it was an official court document or not. I knew it was time to leave. Once you had trouble from country people back then it really didn't matter what your rights were. You had to go because you were a target. It was very easy for someone to sneak up your trailer in the dead of night and set fire to it if they took exception to you. Traveller men would easily stand up for themselves against country folk making trouble for them, but travellers have families and no one wanted to put their women and children in harm's way if it was easier just to move on.

Roseanne, however, understood none of this. In a naive way all she saw was the injustice of being treated no better than a dog. She roused from her sleep in a panic.

'What's going on, Paddy?' she asked. 'What do those men want?'

'Get your stuff together and pack everything away quickly, we're moving out,' I told her. I knew the drill by then.

Outside there was a tussle between a bailiff and a traveller. I went out to help and swung at the man who was pushing my friend around. Before I knew it two other bailiffs were tussling with me.

Roseanne was at the door of our trailer in her dressing gown. She was screaming at the scene unfolding before her.

'Leave him alone, he's done nothing wrong,' she demanded.

I broke free of the men and walked back to the trailer telling them that we were going.

'Why do we have to go anywhere?' Roseanne asked. 'We haven't done anything wrong and we're not doing anyone any harm.'

'It's just the way it is,' I told her.

'But that's not fair,' she sobbed. 'Who are they to order us around?'

She couldn't understand that we could just be moved around because someone, somewhere didn't like who we are and had made a complaint against us. Even though we kept ourselves to ourselves there were, and still are, plenty of people who will work themselves up into a frenzy at the mere sight of a traveller and a caravan.

Roseanne kept repeating herself. 'It's not fair,' she sniffed. She was right, it wasn't. But life isn't fair and it was less fair back then.

We drove off that site and found somewhere else to stay. That night Roseanne was still upset.

'I don't want to be scared in my own home,' she told me. 'I'm still just a girl.'

I held her face in my hands and looked in her eyes. True enough she was young and inexperienced. But she was a wife now, and she had a husband and a new life.

'You're not a girl any more, my Roseanne,' I told her. 'You are a woman, you're my woman.'

From that day that's what I called her: 'Woman'. I'd call out 'woman' when I wanted her and the name stuck.

9

My Patrick

'We're going to have a baby.'

The words hung in the air of the trailer. I blinked, looked at Roseanne and grinned.

'Woman,' I laughed. 'I'm going to be a daddy!'

I grabbed her by the waist and spun her round. She was giggling and trying not to knock into things. There was barely enough room in the trailer to swing a cat, let alone a woman with child. For my Roseanne to be expecting was a glorious thing. We had not even been married six months and already we were going to be blessed with a child. I was the happiest man alive.

When Roseanne got pregnant I knew it was time for a bigger trailer. We'd outgrown our first home already. I had been using the van my father bought me to collect scrap and had also been working the tarmac with Old Quinn and had continued to save.

The trade in trailers is controlled by a few trustworthy men in the traveller world. Your home is the most important and valuable thing you own so the man who sells it to you needs to be equally trustworthy. Travellers have no need for estate agents and you do not need a surveyor to look over a trailer for you. You get to know what to look for and what to look out for. When I bought our second home I had already learnt the hard way to make sure the seals around the windows were water tight and to check for holes.

I went to a dealer man who happened to be a cousin of mine. His name was Blondie Simey on account of his fair hair and he was my father's first cousin. He dealt in trailers and horses. Blood is a trustworthy tie for gypsies so I knew Blondie would not rip me off and would give me a fair deal. For the home I wanted I needed a four-wheel trailer. It would need a bed area for Roseanne, the baby and me. I found what I was looking for on Blondie's lot and gave it a careful going over. I was trading in my old trailer and needed an extra three grand for the new one. It was a lot of money for me at the time but I couldn't raise a family in what I had, so I agreed the price with a handshake.

Blondie didn't take the money off me there and then. 'Give it to me when you've got it Paddy,' he said. 'There's no rush.'

For him, a handshake was as good as a contract, in fact, it meant more. A contract is just a piece of paper. But when you shook on something you gave your word and staked your repu-tation on it. Reputation was everything. If you lost it you lost your standing in the community. No true traveller would ever rip off another traveller.

I hooked the new trailer up to my van and drove off without parting with a penny. A few weeks later I gave Blondie the money and whenever I needed a new trailer after that I always went back to him. Getting your turnout up to how you wanted it was like trading up in cars. I started with a tiny old second-hand model but they got bigger and better, with more chrome, more curtains and more room.

Nowadays trailers are more static that they were back then. It's much harder to travel than it used to be. Gypsies are kept on authorised sites and the trailers stay on the site too. Back then we were more mobile. We would go from camp to camp and take our home with us. There were no beds, there were bunks that we would pull out instead, with leather or cloth covers. In the seventies leather was all the style and I still prefer a leather sofa now.

The mobility that travelling life allowed meant it was much easier for a person to make a living in those days. I was lucky. I had the gift of making money. I would always find a way of getting work or discovering an angle. I could price up scrap in my head and I knew what was worth selling on and what was best left behind. You could cover me in shit and I'd come out smelling of roses. God's been very good to me like that and I was always good at saving money too.

Right up until the birth, neither of us knew whether we were having a son or a daughter. We are both Catholics and we didn't believe in finding out. Whatever we had would be God's will. Roseanne was looked after by St Mary's Hospital in Manchester. Traveller women went to hospital to have their babies just like everyone else, and when it came time for the baby to be born I drove her there. She was anxious and nervous. I was excited.

The midwife led her into the delivery room and I stayed outside in the corridor, nervously pacing and waiting for news. Traveller men don't believe in being there when the baby is born.

We don't cut the cord like country men do these days. That's better off left to the doctors and the professionals. We don't even talk about things like that. Birth and babies and all the medical stuff that goes with it is for women. You won't ever see a traveller at an antenatal class learning breathing exercises. Only sausages do things like that. It's fine for other folk but it's not the traveller way and I doubt whether most traveller wives would want their men in the room with them while they are giving birth. Why would you want to see something like that? If I saw my wife giving birth I'd never look at her that way again. Sex would go out the window. What would I want to look at a thing like that for?

In the waiting area of the maternity ward I couldn't hear or see what was going on inside the room Roseanne was in. I was there with several other anxious dads-to-be. It was 1978 and still not that common for men to be in the room when their wives were giving birth. Every few minutes a midwife or doctor would come and call out a name. I'd look up hopefully. The time passed slowly but eventually a doctor came striding down the corridor. 'Paddy Doherty?' he called.

'That's me,' I said.

'Congratulations, you've had a boy,' he said. 'Mother and baby are doing fine.'

I'll never forget what happened next. As the words sunk in a record came over the loudspeakers in the waiting room. It was 'Love Is In The Air', by John Paul Young. It had been popular the year before. The words couldn't have been more apt.

I asked the doctor how Roseanne was and he said she was fine and that she was resting.

'You can come back in a few hours and see her,' he said.

Hospitals stuck to strict visiting hours in those days. Although it is not customary for traveller men to be in the room when their children are being born, it is customary for them to be in the pub after the birth and so that's what I did. I called my family from the payphone in the hospital. I'd gone from not drinking at all to having a few pints on special occasions and as the birth of my first son was a special occasion we went to wet the baby's head.

After a few hours I made my way back to the hospital to meet my son for the first time. Roseanne was sitting up in bed cradling him. Her smile soon turned to scorn when I walked in.

'Get out, you stink of ale,' she said.

'Come on, woman,' I said. 'I've been celebrating. Show me my son.'

I looked at my baby for the first time and felt a rush like I haven't felt since. He was a handsome child, God bless him. It was the greatest feeling and sometimes now I get sad to think I'll never have that thrill again. I can't describe what it was like to look down at my son in my arms for the first time. I knew that, whatever I went through in life, I owned him, no one else did; he was a bit of me and I owned every bit of him. Those feelings tapped into my past. As a kid I had always belonged to everyone else and no one at the same time. Before I was 17 I had had six parents: Mummy and Daddy, Maggie and Davey Quinn and the Old Man and the Old Queen. My son was all mine. He wouldn't have to spend his life rootless like I had and he wouldn't feel that sense of isolation. He had one daddy and one mummy and that's all he'd ever have. I vowed that Roseanne and I would never leave each other, no matter what happened and what harm came to us, I would make sure we were together until we died so my kids wouldn't have to go through what I went through. I thanked God for giving me a son.

It had never entered my head how I would feel. I'd won the lottery, the pools and I'd won the jackpot. I was a multi-billionaire, I was the richest man on the planet, that's how I felt. I could lift the world and spin it around and roll it away. All because he was mine, I owned him.

He was my double, he had black hair and he had a big dimple in his chin.

As I stood there, gazing down at him asleep peacefully in his blanket, another thought suddenly hit me.

'Fuck, what do we call him?' I said to Roseanne. We looked at each other as the dilemma sunk in.

Traveller tradition dictates that you call your first-born son after his paternal grandfather, my father. But I had three daddies: Dudley Ward, Davey Quinn and Simey Doherty. Who was I supposed to name him after? Whoever I named him after, I was going to upset two of the other men in my life. The thought really troubled me and over the following days our son had no name while we wrestled with the problem.

I wanted to call him Simey, and his name should have been Simey, but I didn't want arguments and I didn't want to offend Dudley or Davey Quinn because they were like fathers to me too. I knew my mother Maggie would want me to call him Davey and Ellen would want me to call him Dudley. I loved them all equally. I didn't want one to have the better of the other but by trying to be fair I couldn't win. The pressure of it was awful. It was worse than getting a beating and it kept me awake at nights. It should have been the happiest period of my life, and in many ways it was, but the name problem hung over me like a dark cloud.

It took the brains of a woman to come up with the solution. In a spark of genius Roseanne said to me: 'I'll take the decision. We'll call him after my dad Patrick.'

'Good idea,' I said, 'it really sounds like he is being named after me.'

'Yes, but who's to know? Put all the blame on me,' she said.

She could see how troubled I was by the whole affair and didn't want it spoil our lives any longer.

With a son to provide for I pushed myself even harder. I had even more of a reason to earn money and be successful and to prove to people that I could be a proud Doherty like my father. I was out six days a week working and wouldn't come home until late. I would get back black with oil, tarmac and dirt from a day's graft.

I looked forward all day to getting home to my family. In the evenings I used to love playing with Patrick, it was the only chance I had to spend time with him. I couldn't get enough of him. With him I was making up for everything I didn't have in my childhood and everything I wanted to have. He got things no traveller had ever had; he had a baby three-wheeler motorbike when they first came out. He had gold chains and bracelets, the best of everything.

At night Patrick slept in the bed with Roseanne and me. He slept in the middle and I would lie there listening to the sound of his breathing and the rain on the roof and think that I was the luckiest man in the world. I used to love cuddling my child and my woman with the wind rocking us to sleep. I knew I was going to invest everything I had in the world in my first-born son. I was going to make him better than I ever was, he would have more than I ever had. I was going to make him into a great fighting man and a great man to earn a living. I was going to make sure he had nothing but the best cars, the best trailers and the best life. I called him my little black fella because he was so dark. We were going to have a fantastic life together. Everything was going to be perfect.

10

Up in Smoke

Knowing when to move on had become instinctive. I got itchy feet when it was time for change and as I watched Patrick grow in those first months I felt a pull away from Manchester and the north. We were approaching a new decade and the country was in a rut. It was getting harder to make money in the north. To be able to provide for Patrick and Roseanne in the way I wanted I needed to stretch my wings and I needed a bigger city to operate in. All roads led to London and the possibilities it held for an up-and-coming entrepreneur.

The opportunities in the capital for travellers were, and still are, better than anywhere else in the country. There are more people to do business with and there are more ways to make money. If you make it in London, you can make it in any city in the nation. The travellers there are a different breed. They are arrogant, they are cocky and they have a point to prove.

There were more opportunities to fight there too, both with country men and travellers. Marriage and fatherhood had briefly slowed down the amount of fighting I had been doing, but I would still gladly get involved with trouble if there was trouble to be had. As a fighter it also took time to suss out a new town and to see where the opportunities were. My reputation was building and I was known in the north but London was far from Manchester and it was a big city.

I'd met many travellers who had moved to London and the city had left a mark on them. Even the Irish travellers who moved there would start talking cockney after a while.

London was a melting pot and one of the first places the Irish and English travellers ever mixed. When I was a kid growing up, integration was unheard of. The two groups lived separate lives and never intermarried. That integration has only happened in the last 25 years. Now my two daughters-in-law are English and it's not an issue at all any more. Back then though it was the lifestyle and culture not to mix. Irish travellers were seen as very rough, they were seen as the lower class. They were better at getting a living and worked harder but the English were fancier; they knew how to do what we call 'word of mouth', they had golden tongues and could talk their way into places and into jobs, whereas the Irish were grafters. There was never bad feeling between the two groups. They just existed separately. In camps the Irish would be on one side and the English on the other, you'd never get them together. Even in the fairs there would be an Irish section and an English section. It's changed now and as far as I am concerned that's a good thing.

The fairs are the places where travellers would meet. There are a few big ones every year like Appleby in Cumbria, Epsom Downs in Surrey and Stow-on-the-Wold. Horse trading was done there and there were rides for the country folk who visited. Back then, the real action for travellers was in the betting schools, the pool tables and the prize-fighting rings. They were the only places where travellers fought other travellers in rings. Sometimes you would arrange to fight specific opponents; other times there would be a resident prizefighter there and you could win £100 if you lasted five rounds with him. You could challenge anyone you wanted and although you fought with gloves on, the gloves didn't have protective stuffing and weighed hardly an ounce.

In one fair, Town Moor near Newcastle-upon-Tyne, I was challenged by a country fighting country man. The stake was £100 and I couldn't refuse. It was just before I moved to London.

A crowd gathered to watch and I had a quiet word in my opponent's ear. He was a big man with a shaved head. I was with Roseanne and our baby and I didn't want trouble but you could never say no to a fight at a fair because there were too many travellers there.

'Listen my friend,' I said, 'it's just a spar. Let's give the crowd a good show and not get carried away.'

'If you can knock me out, fucking knock me out,' he snarled, 'because I'm out to kill you.'

Wonderful, I thought. Another family day out ruined. I knew by the look of the man it wasn't going to be an easy fight and as soon as the bell rang he came at me with a flurry of fearsome shots. He knocked me into the corner. There was a ref there who stayed in the corner and watched with a lazy disinterested look on his face.

I managed to last the first round and towards the end I felt the blows landing on me getting lighter. He's tiring himself out, I thought to myself.

As soon as the bell rang for the second round I ran to him before he had a chance to get up off his stool and laid into him. He went down and I went down on top of him. That roused the ref. He jumped on me and dragged me off with his arm around my neck. The fight was stopped and I was given the £100. I went back to Roseanne, who had been in another part of the fair, with my eye swollen shut and blood dripping from my mouth.

'I won £100,' I said proudly.

'Oh Paddy, what have you done to yourself, you fool?' she fussed. She hated me getting into scraps.

The nearest fair to London was Epsom. It was held during Derby week at the race course. The ring there was made of scaffold poles and was tiny. It was in a part of the fair near a pub called the gambling school. If you fought in that ring there was no dancing around, it was nose-to-nose combat.

The money that changed hands on the pool tables was huge. I once saw someone win £2,800 on a single game and back then that was a huge amount of cash. There was also a game called Pitch Toss that was played with two pennies where major money was won and lost on the toss of the coin. I saw one man walk into Epsom fair as the proud owner of a new Mercedes, a new lorry and a new trailer and after three days at the fair, he, his wife and baby left with nothing. He lost it all.

Travellers from London would return to the north with

stories about the opportunities and schemes in the south which would widen the eyes of impressionable listeners. A little while before I met Roseanne I had stayed in the capital briefly with my dad so I knew the stories were true. I liked the buzz of the city, so when Patrick was around six months old I decided it was time to return there and see what business there was for me.

We moved to Woolwich in south-east London initially and by then I had a lorry and started to work the scrap. The area was full of scrapyards. You would go out on your rounds, load up as much as you could find and then go to one of the yards to weigh it in and sell it. The yards were huge sprawling sites; some were marked out by towers of wrecked cars jutting out of the ground like metal fingers.

Traffic ran in and out of them all day. There was constant loading and unloading and most of the business coming in and out of them was from travellers. We were all in the rat race together, trying to find the opportunities before each other. I soon realised that if I wanted to make serious money, I'd need to come up with a scheme that would give me an edge over everyone else.

The flash of inspiration came one day when I was talking to a man who owned a car scrapyard. In every one I'd been to there was always a pile of tyres.

'What do you do with these?' I asked.

'Nothing we can do, mate, they're worthless,' he said.

It was the days before recycling and any tyres that couldn't be sold as part-worn or remoulded had no value.

However, in most tyres, there was a steel rim and a steel mesh called a radial built into the rubber. Theoretically, they were worth money but it was locked away inside the tyre.

I had an idea. 'I'll take them off you,' I told the man.

'You can have them for nothing,' he said.

I loaded the lorry up with a few tyres and went for a drive, collecting a can of petrol on the way. I was looking for a bit of wasteland that was sheltered and remote. I found what I was looking for in an old derelict factory by the Thames. I pulled the lorry into a corner of it, unloaded the tyres, covered them in petrol then lit them. They went up with a *whoosh* and I waited there for a few minutes just to make sure they caught properly.

As I drove off I looked in the rear-view mirror and saw a column of black smoke rising into the sky. I had only experimented with three or four tyres but the smoke was already visible from the surrounding area. I realised I would have to work at night for my plan to work.

I went to a café, had some lunch, and then a few hours later returned to the scene of the fire. The tyres had melted away into piles of ash and lumps of molten, hardened rubber. What remained was the still-hot steel skeleton inside them. I smiled to myself. I'd hit the jackpot. If I could burn enough tyres, I would have a never-ending supply of free steel.

I spent the next few days driving around east London and the Thames estuary looking for suitable sites and making a note of each one. There was no shortage of remote derelict industrial land in the east of London at the time. My requirements had to be very specific. Access to the site needed to be restricted or easy enough for me to place a restriction across, such as a concrete block or a makeshift barrier. For safety reasons I needed to find locations well away from people or property.

When I'd found enough sites I set Operation Tyre Pyre into full swing. I'd spend the days collecting lorry loads of free tyres from across London. I filled the lorry to the brim with them. Then I'd drive around and build pyres with them in the sites I'd selected and when night fell I drove between the sites with cans of petrol setting light to each pile. The next day, when I'd checked the coast was clear, I returned to pick up the steel to sell. It was a beautiful scheme.

On any given night I'd have piles of tyres burning all over London and when I went to the yards I'd look for the biggest tyres of the lot. I'd be hauling great big tractor wheels onto the back of the truck like an idiot. But I didn't care, I was doing it every day and every night the fires would go up.

I'd try my best to mash up the steel so the yards I sold it to didn't cotton on to what I was doing. Not that it would have mattered to them but I didn't want other travellers knowing the secret because once they did, word would spread and soon everyone would be doing it. You had to be a bit wise and a bit secretive. I was literally making money from nothing, I didn't want everyone else ruining it for me. It was gold dust and it only worked as long as no one else knew about it.

The fire were always set well away from anywhere where they could do harm and it was in the days before people were worried about pollution and carbon dioxide. I had London sewn up for tyres for several months. I was getting away with murder and I loved it.

But eventually copycats started. People got wise to it and then every traveller started doing it. The fire brigade realised too. It became so frequent that the police had to take it more seriously and at that point I had to weigh up the risks against the profits and decided it was time to look for another way of making money.

At the time my father was in living in Croydon and he knew what I was up to.

'Would you stop what you are doing, son?' he'd say.

To him it wasn't a good way to make a living. He was a tarmac man but I didn't want to go into that. I didn't want to go door knocking again. I wanted money there and then; I didn't want to have to slog all day every day. I wanted a guaranteed income.

The next scheme I came up with was much simpler than the tyre fires. I was waiting in a scrapyard one day with a load to sell and no one came out so I started walking around. In the end I was there for an hour and still no one approached me. Other lorries were coming and going and no one seemed to be checking them either. At one point I even climbed in one of the cranes, which had the keys left in it. I thought to myself, 'I could load up here and drive off and no one would be any the wiser.' It happened a few times. I'd go in a yard with a load and just be left there. I would drive around and if anyone looked I would just wave and they'd wave back. As long as you looked like you were meant to be there, no one bothered you. So one day I drove into a yard with an empty lorry and loaded it up with scrap. I made sure I didn't load past the sideboards so when I drove out no one could see what I was carrying. Then I drove out the gates and up the road to the nearest yard where I'd weigh in and sell what I'd taken.

At that time, scrapyards were all run by dodgy people. There was little control over what was going in or coming out of them. Most were fronts for other less legitimate businesses. Doing business with them was a gamble in itself and most of the people working in them would rip you off given half the chance. So I decided to rip them off instead. I would go to scrapyards and see what they had. Then I'd take from one and sell to the other. It was all waste anyway and no one ever checked. I never broke in; I drove my lorry in. It was simple. I was rarely questioned and I did it for months. I could load up in five minutes. I looked for the hidden corners of the yards around the bends. The men who worked in them were inevitably lazy and would never leave their huts or Portakabins to walk all the way over to see what was going on. It was so easy it was unbelievable and yet no one ever thought of doing it.

If anyone ever did stop me I would just tell them I was going to get the load weighed to see how much it cost. The worst that would happen was that they'd bar me. There were a million scrapyards so it didn't matter and most were so dodgy they didn't want the police sniffing around. I got barred from seven or eight yards. It was a victimless crime.

Roseanne was blissfully unaware that any of this was happening, even when I returned home late at night black with soot and stinking of rubber smoke. I would never tell her where the money came from. She would ask but I'd just give her a pile of notes and tell her to put it away. She was in control of the finances and the saving. I would keep a little back for myself, I'd always have a bit of cash in my pocket and she'd never know how much, but the majority of it went in the savings jar. She'd always tell me how much was in the kitty and she'd tell me at the end of the week how well we'd done.

Despite the easy money schemes I still had a strong work ethic. I was just seduced by the ease of it all. It was the time of *Only Fools and Horses* where everyone was looking for a way to make a quick pound. Travellers never believed in training for things at that time and I learnt trades like tarmacking on the job. If there was tarmac work I'd still get out there with my father and do as much as I could. I was freaky-like, I loved to graft.

Within a few months of moving to London my reputation began to spread around the city. There were organised fights happening all over London, usually at dawn on a Sunday morning. There were areas where they took place; specific car parks and parks that travellers knew about. There was one called the Scrubs in Hammersmith, it was a field at the back of a park which was shielded from view. The cops would know where the fights were happening and they knew how big the organised fighting scene was but they didn't want anything to do with it. Their attitude was 'let them sort it out themselves'. Men got injured all right, sometimes very badly, but I never heard of a traveller dying through a bare-knuckle fight because before it got to that stage the fair play man would stop it.

Outside of the traveller fights I had my own little wars as well. It seemed I couldn't go in a pub without someone taking exception to me and wanting to prove themselves against me. When you fought country people there were no rules and anything went. I had a minor argument with a man in a pub in London the day before I was due to have an organised fight. He'd been slagging off gypsies and I told him to keep his mouth shut. When I went to leave he was waiting behind a pillar for me with a pool cue. As I walked past he swung it straight into my mouth. That's all I remember. I went down on the ground with a thud. When I woke I saw the pool cue lying next to me and tasted blood in my mouth. I felt my teeth and I couldn't believe that they were all still there. I went back home and Roseanne opened the door, saw the state of me and started crying. When she calmed down she cleaned me up and fussed over me.

'You can't fight tomorrow, look at the state of you,' she said.

But I couldn't back out, that would have been too shameful. I wasn't bothered about a split lip and bruising anyway, what bothered me more was the clicking noise in my ears each time I spoke. Something had happened to my jaw.

'I am still fighting in the morning,' I told her and the next day I headed out to a car park behind Tottenham police station where a lot of fights took place under the nose of the cops. It was a summer morning at 5 a.m.; fighting time. There was no one around except for travellers and the sun was coming up. It was like an old-fashioned duel.

I knew my opponent well and we respected each other enough not to have a fair play man there, which was rare. We would both abide by the rules. The fight started and I was jeering him to rile him up. Each time I spoke I could hear the noise in my ear coming from my jaw. I felt the searing pain but it didn't distract me. I was single-minded in my pursuit of victory. I had learnt early in life to ignore pain. I was knocked down twice but got up and gave as good as I got. Then he threw a thundering hook that connected with my chin. I heard a sickening crack and I knew instantly that my jaw had broken. It was shattered and I knew I had no choice but to go for it and try and knock my opponent out. It wasn't in me to give best to him but I was injured so I needed to finish the fight.

His blow had knocked me to the floor.

'Stay down there as long as you want,' my opponent laughed.

I got back up and dropped him with a straight right in the face.

As he got up I saw the cut on his eye and knew I was in with a chance. When you cut someone the flesh around it gets tender like meat and you can work on it and really open it up.

We were trading blows toe-to-toe. He was about six stone heavier than me and I knew at first that I couldn't afford to stand with him, he would have beaten me, but as it went on and he got tired I knew he would weaken. My jaw was aching and the pain was unnatural. I could feel every clout I received reverberating through the snapped bone. It was like being hit with a hammer and I knew I couldn't stand there and fight for much longer so I willed myself to drop him.

I got right into him. He had to fight hard to keep me away. We laid into each other and it seemed that neither would give way. Fate intervened when an elderly couple drove into the car park in a Mini Metro.

They saw what was going on and wound down the window of their car. 'We're going to get the police,' they called. I actually laughed, because we were so near the station.

Nobody wanted trouble and as soon as there was a sniff of the law fights were over. We didn't even have to discuss it, we both knew the fight was over for the time being and we shook hands and decided to settle it another day.

By the time I got home I could hardly speak. I could hear the bone flopping around in my jaw. Roseanne squealed when she saw the state of me and told me to get straight to hospital. I couldn't talk and my tongue was swelling up.

By the time I got to A & E I was in agony and I could tell by the look on the doctor's face that it was serious. I was rushed straight into X-ray but I didn't need an expert to tell me that both sides of my jaw had been completely dislocated and shattered. My mouth was only held shut by tendon and muscle.

The previous night in the pub, the pool cue had fractured the bone and that day the punch had shattered it where it had already weakened. I had to go in for an operation that day and the surgeons needed to reconstruct my jawbone. They put metal screws in each jaw to reattach them to my skull and joined them across the chin with a titanium plate. Since then I've had my jaw broken another five times and today all my mouth and jaw is metal.

Fights started for small reasons. A fighter knew how to start one. It's all to do with blackguarding; jeering, taking the piss. But with travellers it can be much more subtle than just abusing someone. People would know what buttons to press. Anyone who called me 'little' Paddy Doherty – I was always sensitive about my height and would be looking for a fight. At that time I had something to prove and to me that was an insult. They'd also know of my family background and call me a black bastard, or purposely call me Paddy Ward. People would say it and they'd know it would wind me up. As far as I was concerned they were calling me out and I'd rise to it, whether they meant harm by it or not.

But once the fight was finished, the beef was over. I would batter someone in a fight, see them the next week in the pub with their family and buy them a drink. Once it was over there was nothing to be annoyed about. You sorted out your problem, shook hands and it was forgotten. The reason for the fight would never come up in conversation again and if someone did bring it up they would be told to shut up.

All my opponents were enemies until the fight was done. I often had fights with people I knew and respected. It was a way of life for me. Violence was both a hobby and a career and I was beginning to believe I was indestructible.

11

Family Fortunes

I was afraid of nothing. I knew pain, I got hurt and I bled just like everyone else, but it never bothered me. Pain seemed normal and I knew no fear. Sometimes I welcomed hurt. I took beatings and I gave beatings and I never felt more alive than when I was half dead and on the ropes, fighting with every ounce of my heart and will.

Perhaps it was because of all those beatings when I was young but I truly believed I was immune to death.

It was a different story for my loved ones though. When Patrick was less than two years old he developed a cough that didn't go away. He'd cry and squirm as the coughing fits took hold of him and no amount of medication would ease him. It seemed to go on for weeks and weeks and Roseanne and I became increasingly concerned. When his temperature shot up we knew he needed more than just antibiotics and took him to A & E. He had been such a lively, happy baby but by the time we got him to hospital even the crying had stopped. He was listless and quiet and he was struggling to breathe. He was admitted straight away and after hurried tests was placed into a high dependency unit.

'I'm sorry, Mr and Mrs Doherty, but your son has pneumonia and pleurisy,' we were told.

I knew that pneumonia was potentially deadly and I didn't know what pleurisy was but the doctor explained that it was inflammation of the lungs and that it would be hurting Patrick every time he breathed. The thought that my baby son was in pain and in danger tortured me and I would have gladly given my life for his at that point in time.

'Be strong my little man,' I told him as he lay in his hospital cot. There were tubes connected up to him and he had an oxygen line under his nose to help him breathe. He was given stronger medicine, painkillers and put on a drip because he hadn't been eating.

He was kept in the hospital in Hackney in east London for over a week and Roseanne and I kept vigil by his bedside. At night I would sit and watch his chest rise and fall fitfully and pray to God that he would get better. I'd never before felt the love I felt for Patrick. I wouldn't allow myself to think dark thoughts that he would die. But every so often a wave of panic would rise in my chest and I'd have to will it away before it engulfed me.

After around four days my prayers were beginning to be answered. Patrick was responding to the treatment and the colour was coming back to his little body, which had been so pale it was almost blue when we took him in. He started babbling again and when Roseanne picked him up and tickled him he would smile.

He was moved out of intensive care and put on a ward with other children. One day when we were with him a photographer came to the ward and asked us if we wouldn't mind having

Patrick's picture taken. The man explained that it was for a local newspaper bonny baby competition.

We laughed. 'Of course you can,' we agreed.

The next week when Patrick was out of hospital and at home we bought the newspaper and eagerly turned to the page with the hospital children on it. And there was our Par, as we called him, the winner, the bonniest baby of them all.

My goal became to make Par a rich man. I wanted him to have everything I didn't. Travellers want the best for their sons; they want them to better their family name. I didn't care if I was poor and had nothing as long as he was very rich. I didn't care how I did it; rob, steal or beg, I would make him a rich man and I would make him brainy too.

Soon after our scare Roseanne fell pregnant again. It was perfect news. Patrick was well and healthy and we were expanding our family.

Once again when it was time for the birth we did not know whether we were having a boy or a girl and once again I stayed outside the room while Roseanne had our baby.

When the doctor came out and told me I'd had another son I was overjoyed. I was the man. I had two sons and in traveller culture the more sons you have the better. Boys are doted on by everyone.

Naming our baby this time was easier. We had already got over the issue of how to name the first but the new male addition to the family had to be called Simey after my father. There was no discussion. Simey Doherty was born with a mop of light hair. I could tell the minute I set eyes on him that the women in the family would love him. I don't know why but traveller women bond with blond babies and Simey was a fair little boy.

We'd returned to Manchester to have him and after some discussion we decided to stay in the north. I did well out of London, we lived there for two years, but money-making opportunities were getting tighter in the capital, so I wasn't too sad to leave. The scrapyards had cottoned on to my scheme and would phone each other when they knew I was around. I liked London life but Roseanne never settled, and she wanted to be near her family when she had her second child, so we moved to a trailer in Oldham. Oldham would be a fresh start.

My reputation came with me however and in each new place I went I would never hide the fact that I was a Doherty and I was a fighter. I was doing well in business and had made some decent money so we began to enjoy days out and holidays. Even on family breaks trouble seemed to find me.

When Patrick and Simey were young we were in Brighton one summer with my cousins Joe, Paddy and Tommy Mary. I was with the children, my brothers David and Dudlow, and our women. We were all in a pub enjoying a quiet drink when an argument started over a game of pool between David and another man.

My brother David is nicknamed 'Shout' because he can't talk quietly. He means no harm by it but some folk take exception. David was being fronted up by the man he was playing and was shouting at him. The man, who happened to be much bigger than David, wanted to take him outside and batter him.

We were just six travellers in a pub that was packed full of non-travellers. They all appeared to know each other. I'd been used to hostile looks all my life so it meant nothing to me to walk in a place and feel unwelcome, but once the argument broke out I knew straight away there was going to be trouble. I knew what was going to happen and it would involve all us travellers getting attacked. David must have known this too because he backed away a bit and even quietened down. But out of the corner of my eye I saw the landlord lock the door and I knew we were going to get it. We weren't going to be allowed out of the pub without some nasty consequences.

Someone had made a call and within a few minutes as I was trying to calm the argument three cars pulled up outside and loads of heavies got out. I pulled David back. I'd mixed with enough country folk to know what was happening.

This could end seriously. Our women were nervous and Roseanne had gathered the children to her and was looking at me with a grave expression on her face. I knew I could handle myself, but I wasn't on my own, and I couldn't let my woman and my boys get in harm's way. I knew what I had to do.

'Shut up and let me do the talking,' I said to my brother and approached the man he had been shouting at who appeared to be the ringleader.

'What's your problem?' he spat at me.

'Forget you and my brother,' I said. 'It's a hundred to one here, we're not going to get out of here, so who is the best man in this pub? Let me and him go outside in the car park and have a one-to-one. No dirty tricks, a fist fight, win lose or draw we'll shake hands, knock it on the head and everyone can go home.'

The man thought about it for a minute and then pointed out another fellow. He was full of muscle, he looked the bollocks and he had hands like shovels.

'For fuck's sake!' I said under my breath. But me getting a hiding was better than the whole lot of us coming to harm.

I went outside with this ape of a man and the pub cleared out as everyone followed. Roseanne was weeping and tugging at my arm. 'Don't do it Paddy,' she was begging.

But there was no chance of me backing down.

Me and the big guy stripped off down to our waists and when he took off his top his abs looked like they'd been carved from stone. I was impressed. It was in the days before bodybuilding and steroids; he must have worked hard to look like he did.

The minute he put his hands up I knew his reach would be too long and if I stayed back and tried to jab he would knock my head off. I had to get into him.

He knocked me over with the first punch he threw that connected cleanly.

'Get up, you wanker,' he said.

I got up, took another few shots and he dropped me again. My mouth was split open and I was swallowing my own blood. I'd got used to the taste over the years, it was no problem.

I knew I needed to slip inside his reach so as he was sending me another letter I ducked under his arm into his chest and lifted my head as hard and fast as I could. I caught him under his chin. It was a clean shot and he went down straight away. The plan had worked beautifully.

He got up and I knew by his face his bottle had gone. He could give it but he couldn't take it.

All the country men crowding round were shouting to him. 'Give it to the Irish tosser,' they were baying.

Their hatred inspired me, it made me want to beat him more and I knew I had him.

The next punch he threw I did the same again and I almost smiled as I heard his chin crack when my head connected with it. His legs wobbled and he started to go over. He was blinking, stunned, and I caught him on the way down with an uppercut.

'Night, night,' I laughed.

He was in no state to carry on. 'I've had enough,' he whimpered. His face started to swell, like it was being inflated with a tyre hose. His chin looked misshaped.

It was short and brutal and it was over.

'Right we'll be off then,' I said and thanked the man in charge for giving me his word. Manners cost nothing after all.

'How did you beat him?' he asked.

'Ask him,' I said pointing to the bloodied mess on the ground.

We got in our cars and went back to the site. Half an hour later the police came. They had been alerted by someone in the pub to what had happened and said they wanted to check if we were okay. It was bred into me not to talk or collude with them so when they asked me who was fighting I told them I didn't know, even though I had a fat lip and was still bleeding.

After fights my name went out further again. Travellers are awful people for exaggerating things. After that one the rumour was that Paddy Doherty beat a man who had been seven feet tall,

18 stone and rippled with muscles. True, he was a big man but not that big.

I developed a knack for being able to read a fight as well as an opponent. The minute I got one clout, I would know whether I was in for a hard fight, a long fight or a 50-50 fight. I would know from the first contact whether I could beat him easily and be able to torture and play with him. I never once went into a fight thinking I would lose.

A year after Simey was born we were expecting a baby again. Our plan of having a big family was working well. Roseanne had been brilliant during each pregnancy and she was a natural mother. She was everything you wanted in a wife. She was devoted and caring and she looked after the children and the home while I went out to work.

With our third child we were blessed with a daughter. Naming her was easy, she was called Margaret, after Maggie and after Roseanne's mother. Everyone was happy. It felt different having a daughter after the two boys but it was wonderful. While Patrick was my hopes and dreams, and while Simey would follow his brother's example, I knew that Margaret was destined one day to get married and break my heart. I would always be her daddy and I felt a tug of protectiveness when I held her. She was my little girl; she was her daddy's princess. If I had known then what I know now, that I would only ever have one surviving daughter, I wouldn't have cared about honouring my mother and my mother-in-law with her name, I would have called her Roseanne straight away.

12

Life and Death

The eighties were good to me. The recession gave way to boom and business went from strength to strength. I was at the prime of my life and I was doing okay. I had money and status and I was everyone's friend. And by 1988 there had been two more additions to the family, my sons David and Johnny.

Our life still revolved around travelling. We moved all over the country and never stayed anywhere for more than 18 months. Roseanne and I would relax by going to the pictures and on Saturdays we'd sometimes go to a club. When we were in London we'd go to the Hammersmith Palais. There would be about ten fights a night there, one of them usually involved me. There was a café across the road and I would fight in the car park then go back in to the dance. It became part of a normal night out. Fighting was in my nature.

I kept the extent of my fighting career from Roseanne. She knew I got into scrapes and she hated it. When I'd leave early in a Sunday morning to go and fight I wouldn't have to tell her where I was going. She always knew and she worried. She'd seen me bloodied and bruised several times and she'd try and talk me out of it. It was easier not to tell her. I couldn't turn a fight down because of who I was. I had too much pride in myself to turn down an opportunity. Roseanne understood, but it was still hard for her.

Away from fighting I was a family man and devoted to my children. I gave them everything I never had in life and more. Every one of them had a silver spoon in their mouth... in fact, it wasn't silver, it was gold. I spoiled them; they were my life. I had it all worked out for them. I wanted Patrick to follow me in that part of the family business. Simey grew up to love horses and was always good at spotting ones that could be bought and sold on for a profit, even when he was a kid. He was quieter and more thoughtful than his older brother. I taught him the horse trade and we went to horse fairs as a family. In the north the big event was Appleby. The horse fair there was a huge affair for travellers and thousands descend on the village every year. And there was a regular horse auction in Southall in west London that I went to sometimes as well when I was in the capital. Horses are in our blood and I'd go out with the kids and drive with a trap at the weekend. It was a family interest handed down from generation to generation. My old man knew the horse trade well. He was called 'the Blacksmith' because he used to shoe horses.

All my kids were loved but there was a special place in my heart for Patrick. I loved them all; if one hurt, I felt the pain. But Patrick was my first-born, so when I died he was going to be the head of the family. Travellers put extra stock in their first-born sons. I'm sure country people do too, they just don't like to admit it.

My David was born in 1984 and my Johnny was born in 1988 and when he was less than a year old Roseanne was pregnant again. It was the way our life was becoming; every year or two we would have a new member of the family. I can never understand why people have small families. Life is about making life and carrying on your name, and that's what we were doing.

We'd been blessed with all our children. We had five and each birth had gone smoothly with no complications. Although we never took the blessing of a child for granted and always gave thanks, we'd almost become blasé. Roseanne went for the scans, they were always fine and then life carried on as normal. We never asked to know whether the child was a boy or a girl and didn't this time either. Everything in the pregnancy was normal, there was no indication of trouble and so, when it was time for the baby to come, we were both relaxed when we headed to St Mary's Hospital in Manchester again.

I was familiar with the waiting room by then. I'd been going there for 11 years as, with each birth, wherever in the country we were living, Roseanne insisted on returning to Manchester. She was like a salmon going home to spawn!

I took my usual seat in the waiting area. Times had changed. When Patrick was born the room was full of fathers. But it was 1989 when baby number six came along. The most popular picture in the country was a poster of a man with his shirt off holding a baby. Everyone was talking about the 'new man' and men were being encouraged to show their sensitive sides. It was common for men to be at the birth of their children. Apparently, country men were getting in touch with their feminine sides and getting all sensitive. I don't know if it had anything to do with that poster but there were fewer men in the waiting area than I'd ever seen. I couldn't care less about some bloke cuddling a baby on a poster. There was no way I was going in the room to see my babies being born.

I don't recall how long I was in there waiting but when the doctor found me, I could tell instantly there was something wrong. He didn't even have to talk, I could see by the look in his eyes.

'What's wrong?' I said before he had a chance to speak.

'Mr Doherty, you've had a girl... but there have been serious complications. The baby's heartbeat began to drop so we had to do an emergency C section.'

Immediately my mind turned to Roseanne. I felt a pang of panic. 'Where's my wife, is she okay?'

'Your wife is fine and you can go and see her,' he answered. 'But there is something wrong with your daughter. We are not yet sure what it is but she is in a very serious condition, Mr Doherty. She will not survive.'

His words did not register. My thoughts then were with my wife and I needed to see her and see that she was okay. I ran to her room. She looked drained and distraught. She was holding our baby. Tears were streaming down her face

I laid next to her and looked at our child.

She was a handsome little girl and she looked normal in every way. Her eyes were shut and she was as pale as a cloud. Her skin looked paper-thin, like a sheet of delicate paper, you could see the blue veins laced underneath it.

I didn't know what to say or how to comfort my wife so I sat silently looking at the closed eyes of my newborn daughter as her life slowly ebbed away.

The doctors tried to explain. They said a lot of medical stuff that I didn't understand. I just wanted them all to go away and to be with my wife and child because I knew time together was a luxury we would never have.

We called her Elizabeth and she survived for less than an hour. Her breaths became shallower, she faded away and slowly her movements became imperceptible, until the angels came and claimed her. She never made a sound. She left us in silence. The only sound in the room when she died was the sound of Roseanne quietly sobbing.

We were both in shock. Nothing had indicated that there was anything wrong. The doctors were just as stunned as we were and in the days that followed, after we buried our daughter in Gorton Cemetery, they set about looking for answers.

Eventually the investigation was taken up by geneticists in London. Samples of blood and tissue had been taken from our daughter and they discovered a hidden killer in our cells which had been sitting silently, waiting to be activated. Elizabeth had been born with a condition called Fraser syndrome, a rare genetic condition which almost always proves fatal. Babies born with Fraser syndrome suffer a range of problems; some are born with no kidneys, some with eyelids but no eyes, others are born with webbed fingers and toes, some are born with a layer of skin over their face like a veil. The condition also leads to problems with lungs, liver and the nervous system. If sufferers survive birth, life expectancy is less than a year. The condition affects fewer than one in 10,000 births. Our scans didn't show it up, but to be fair on the doctors, given that we already had five unaffected children, the doctors wouldn't have been looking for it.

We'd been so lucky up to that point and it was a devastating blow. When a child dies the first thing you do is to look for answers. Was it something we had done, could we have done anything to save her? Even after years of hindsight I still have no answers except for the fact that life is fragile and chance turns on the roll of a dice. If it is God's will, there's nothing you can do but accept things as they are.

Although Johnny was just a year old and too young to understand what happened, the other children were upset and confused. We told them that their little sister had gone to be an angel with God.

The doctors explained that there would be a one in three chance of any more babies we had being born with the condition. It was a troubling weight on our minds because we still planned to extend our family and knew that, because of our beliefs about birth control, we would have to let God decide what happened in the future.

A year later Roseanne was expecting again so naturally we were worried. The hospital kept a close eye on the baby and we prayed that it would be healthy. We didn't think we would be unlucky twice in a row. But at 18 weeks Roseanne went for a scan and our hearts were broken once more. It took three doctors to peer at the grainy image on the screen and confirm our worst fears. Our baby had Fraser syndrome.

My heart was empty. Roseanne was crushed and I felt helpless. In life I could always use my fists to fight my way out of a corner and to protect my family, but there was nothing I could do about this. Roseanne was in shock. The doctors doubted our baby would survive in the womb and recommended that Roseanne undergo a termination. That too was totally against our beliefs and so Roseanne carried the child to full term. It was an agonising five months' wait. She convinced herself that the baby would be born and would survive. We prayed every day for a miracle to happen. Roseanne's faith was so strong that she believed that the baby would live as the time came nearer. However, the doctors kept a close eye on the baby and could offer no hope.

'Everything will come right Paddy,' Roseanne would tell me.

But tragedy was to strike twice. Our baby daughter, Helen, was born in September 1990 at 38 weeks. She died shortly after she was born.

The familiar thoughts went through our minds. Why us? What were we being punished for? Again, I had no answers.

The death affected Roseanne much harder this time. She hadn't really stopped grieving for Elizabeth and she fell into a spiral of despair. She couldn't get up some mornings and was weighed down by grief. I can't imagine what it must have been like for her carrying a child she knew in her heart of hearts would die before or soon after birth.

Religion plays a big part in our culture and after we lost our Helen, Roseanne turned to the church once more for comfort. She rediscovered her faith and that helped her get through it. She coped because she once again accepted God and his son Jesus into her life. She went to church more. When it first happened we questioned our faith, but with time we realised that there are tragedies in the world and rather than ask 'why me?', you sometimes have to ask 'why shouldn't it be me, what makes me immune?' You might imagine you turn away from God over a tragedy like that but we didn't, we went to church more and sought comfort in Him.

We buried Helen in Gorton alongside her sister. As I threw a handful of soil onto her casket it seemed to me that the graveyard was beginning to fill with Dohertys.

Another silent killer also stalked my family. My father's side carried the gene for cystic fibrosis. It affected my brother on my father's side, Francey. He succumbed to the condition before his 30th birthday.

Francey was my younger brother but the truth is that in many ways I looked up to him as though he were older than me. It saddens me to think he never really knew that. He would always put me right about things and he didn't care about being blunt. I'd call him for advice. If I fell out with anyone, Francey would not worry about telling me that I was in the wrong. He bowed to no one either except his father and God. If I had an argument with my old man, Francey would smooth things over. He was direct. He wouldn't beat about the bush but he was so wise. He was a peacemaker. When he died, a part of me died with him.

He was well over six foot tall and he never let the illness get him down. He faced the trials of his condition with a bravery you rarely see. Like all his brothers he was a fighter and a great man, in many ways he was the toughest fighter of all of us Dohertys because he was fighting a battle he could never win.

He spent a lot of time in hospital having operations to try and treat and deal with the symptoms of his illness. He was prone to many chest infections and often had difficulty breathing. He lived 200 miles away but I would go and visit him in hospital whenever he was due to have surgery.

One day I went to visit him and he jokingly asked: 'What are you going to do for me while I'm in here, our Pat?' (My father's side of the family always refer to me as Pat or Patrick.)

'I'm going to get your name tattooed on me,' I laughed.

'Are you now?' he said. But the more I thought about it, the more I thought it was a good idea. What better way to show him how much I honoured him. So I drove back to Manchester on the motorway and when I got into town I stopped at the tattoo parlour I used and had his name etched on my arm.

I called him the next day, when he came round from the operation.

'Remember that promise I made you, Francey?'

'Yes, Patrick, I do, are you still going to do that for me?' he said.

'I've gone one better, I got it done that day.'

He didn't believe me. 'Go away,' he laughed.

So the following day I got in the car again and drove 200 miles down the motorway to show him. He wasn't a man to show emotion but I could tell he was pleased.

Francey joined our Nelly, my daddy Dudley Wards's daughter, in heaven. Hers was the first death I remember, she had 13 children. She was in her early thirties when she died. She had an appointment in the hospital and was waiting in the waiting room with my mother. She leaned over to get something and as she did, she suffered a massive heart attack. She died there and then in the seat.

I remember her funeral and all the others since. A traveller funeral is special. It is like no other. There are always hundreds of people because we are extremely respectful to our dead. When a traveller dies, every other traveller wants to pay respects to the departed. Travellers never speak ill of their dead. We honour them and keep their memory alive.

Ellen Ward died in 1989 and we took her back home to Ireland to be buried. It was a huge funeral. We buried her in Dublin with her husband Dudley, who had died in 1982. She too died of a heart attack. I went to the funeral with Roseanne, Patrick, Simey, David and Johnny – who was just a toddler – and my brother Dudlow. Dudlow had a lot of enemies in Ireland and it wasn't long before trouble found us. Word spread quickly that he was going to the funeral and we had only just driven off the boat when we were approached by a man who wanted to arrange a fight.

'I'll meet him in the morning after the funeral,' he demanded.

At the time Dudlow was having problems with his health and was in no fit state to be fighting, even though he was normally more than capable. He was a good fighter but a dirty one. He earned himself the nickname of Rough Dudlow Ward, on account of his habit of pushing the boundaries of fair play when he needed to. In this instance, however, it would not have been fitting for him to fight so I offered to take his place and was told to turn up in a remote country lane the afternoon after the funeral. The funny thing was that even though I was there to bury my mother, it didn't register in my mind that there was anything wrong with getting involved in a fight while I was in Ireland. Fighting is so much a part of the traveller way of life that even at funerals and while grieving our dead it's part of the course.

The following day we went to the chapel for the service and on to the graveyard to bury Mummy. There were hundreds of travellers in attendance, all different breeds from families across Ireland and the UK. Davey Quinn was there with Maggie and he took me aside.

'Paddy, it is our Ellen's funeral. Don't go back and fight,' he said.

As always he was the voice of reason, but although he was giving me wise counsel, in those days my heart ruled my head and I wanted to be the man to sort out Dudlow's problems for him. If someone had thrown down the gauntlet and requested a fight, a fight would take place. Serious fighting travellers didn't worry who they fought as long as the root cause of the argument was settled.

I drove to the fight on the way back to the ferry with all my family in the car. That's how brazen I was. I was single-minded when it came to defending my reputation. I pulled up at the designated spot and was surrounded by travellers who had all turned up, drawn by the gossip that Paddy Doherty was in town and had offered himself up in place of his brother. By now my reputation had crossed the Irish Sea. Fired by the crowd, many of whom were hostile, I got out the car and jumped on the roof. Silence fell and all eyes turned in my direction.

'I'm Paddy Doherty,' I shouted. 'Anyone who wants to fight my brother will have to fight me.'

I waited. The only sound was birdsong and the rustling of feet. No one spoke.

'Well, what's it to be then?' I shouted. 'Which man among you has a problem with my brother?'

No one stepped forward. I looked across at the faces in the crowd and not one of them looked up at me. I sneered and got back in the car. As we drove away the crowd parted to let us through.

Dudlow never forgot what I did for him that day. Afterwards he vowed never to return to Ireland. He wasn't a man for sentiment but the following day I went to his house and he was there drinking without a care in the world. He put his arm around me, kissed me and thanked me. I felt like I'd won the lottery that day because I admired him so much.

The sad irony was that within six months Dudlow was dead. He too died of a heart attack. It was a year filled with tragedy. When Mummy died I finally called Maggie 'mother' for the first time. I could never do it when Ellen was alive because even then, years after I knew Maggie was my mother, I still looked at Ellen as my mummy.

In the summer of 1990 I lost another huge figure in my life. Davey Quinn, the man who raised me as his own son, died. He was just 56 years old.

His death hit me hard. There was an empty space in my life when he passed over. He was ill for seven days before he finally slipped away. I stayed with him all that time. I slept in the corridor and made sure I never ventured far from his hospital bed. He suffered a massive heart attack but he fought it as hard as he could. There was a heatwave at the time which didn't help him. He was in a hospital bed and he had fans all around him to keep him cool. His kidneys began to fail and a week after the first attack he had another smaller one. But there was no fight left in him and that finished him off. I arranged his funeral and made sure he got the send off a great man deserved.

All my life Davey Quinn had never put his hand on me but I still respected him and loved him just the same. We used to have father and son talks and I'd ask his advice. He could sniff out a liar and he knew when people were using me and trying to rip me off. With Old Quinn gone I suddenly felt lost and exposed.

As the eldest man in the Ward family I became head after his death. According to tradition he was mourned for a year. Mother wore black every day. She never even turned a radio on or watched television for 12 months after his death. I don't think I saw her smile or heard her laugh once. She missed him terribly, as we all did. He'd been a huge part of the family and a huge part of all of our lives

A year after his death, his youngest daughter, my sister Julie, got married. It was the first big family celebration since Quinn's death and I was honoured when Julie asked me to give her away. She too had mourned for a year and had waited that time before she said her vows as a mark of respect.

It was an emotional day. There were hundreds of guests but I couldn't help notice all the people who should have been there.

Julie married without any of her grandparents present, or her dad. It seemed that in a very short space of time, a huge chunk had been ripped out of the family.

I was a very proud man when I walked Julie down the aisle. I was 32 and my own daughter was just nine years old. It didn't seem right that I was giving my sister away. I wasn't old enough and as I gave her hand over to her new husband I kept thinking that it should have been Quinn in my place.

13

Fists of Fury

Things had started to change for travellers by the 1990s. It was harder for us to move around, there were big sites provided for us to settle on so more travellers were staying in one place, but there were more opportunities for our children. The underlying prejudices were still there. Most country folk still barely gave us the time of day but the 'no travellers allowed' signs that I had seen in my youth had mostly come down and our children were encouraged to go to school. Not many travellers took advantage of this and many of those that did still removed their children from school before they finished their education.

I had been acutely aware all my life of the disadvantages of not having an education. I still struggled with reading and writing so I made sure all my children went to school. I wanted them to have all the things I never had and to be able to take advantage of all the opportunities. So, although it was unusual at the time, the Doherty children left the site each morning in their school uniforms and went to school. I'm not being disrespectful here, but a lot of travellers were thick and ignorant and they didn't agree with me sending my children to school where they would mix with a lot of country people, but I didn't care what they thought of me as long as my children were getting educated.

There is a saying that sometimes you have to be cruel to be kind and that's how I approached schooling my children. They didn't want to go. Of course they didn't, what child does? And it was equally hard for them because many of the children they knew didn't go to school. However, they knew what awaited them at home if they didn't go. Me! And it was hard for me too. The education system welcomed them and encouraged them to attend classes but once they were there, the old prejudices were still just as apparent in the playground as they were in my school days. I sent my kids to school knowing they would get picked on and bullied because of what they were. When I thought about the way I suffered during my schooldays it broke my heart to think my children might be suffering in the same way. But in my mind we all had to make sacrifices for the greater good. There were no if and buts – even if they were bullied, if they didn't go to school they were not going to be able to read or write and to me that wasn't acceptable. I always made sure I took them to school and picked them up. And on the occasions when we went travelling, tutors would come out to the sites to carry on their education.

I made sure I was always around for my children. They had the best of everything. Each of my sons were enrolled in boxing clubs at 11, just as I had been, and Patrick and Simey would spar together. I kept them fit and they knew the value of hard work. Every Sunday we would go to Mass in the morning at a church several miles away and then run home where Roseanne would have a big breakfast waiting for us. I made sure they ate everything up. It was a special moment when I bought each of them their first boxing gloves and boots.

The children had the best of everything. We'd go swimming together and to the cinema. I loved being a dad and I lived the fantasy childhood I never had through them. With each birth, and with the tragic deaths of our daughters, the tattooed names of my children down my back got longer. I tried to impress on them how important it was to read and write.

In truth, all my children all hated school but I hope now they appreciate that I did the right thing by them. I made them go because I didn't want them to lose what I lost. We'd have rows about it every Monday morning. They'd beg not to go. But eventually they accepted it and although sometimes they did get picked on, they stuck it out and they all finished school. It helped when they were all together because they were able to stick up for each other. They mixed with non-travellers and it widened their view of the world. In my mind that's not a bad thing. I took an active interest in all their educations and I used to go to parents' evening, like the country parents, to make sure they were doing well. And unlike the monsters that I came across when I was a child, their teachers were dedicated and professional. Today I am proud to be able to say that all my sons and my daughter and wife can read and write.

The humiliation of my school days was hard to leave behind me, however. Years after I left school, when things were going great for me and I was making a good living, I remembered one particular teacher, the woodwork teacher at my last school, St John Vianney. He had taken me to one side and had told me that I would make nothing of my life. What sort of teacher does that to a young lad? I knew that now was the time to prove him wrong. I went and bought myself a new Armani suit, some nice shoes, a collar and tie and I went back to the school. In reception I asked for the woodwork teacher and was told that he wasn't there that day. Instead the headteacher, who remembered me, came down to say hello.

'What are you doing back here?' he asked.

'I wanted to see my old woodwork teacher,' I explained. I pointed out the window to my car. It was a flash Bentley, that I had polished to perfection. Its grinning metallic grill was shining in the sun.

'That's my car,' I said. 'It's bought and paid for, it's not on finance. This suit belongs to me. I paid for it, with cash.' The headteacher nodded but looked puzzled.

'Can you just tell that teacher that the boy who he said would never amount to anything and would never go anywhere has done okay for himself and has gone places?' I explained. And with that, I shook the headteacher's hand, walked out to my car and drove out of the school gates.

While my children were pursuing an education, I was pushing myself to attain the perfect turnout. I had the nice cars and the big trailers but I was still chasing more. You see, when it comes to your turnout, you can never be satisfied. There's no such thing as perfection. It can always be improved upon. You will never hear a traveller say, 'I'm doing all right now, I'll settle for this.' It's in our nature to want more and improve ourselves. In traveller culture you are judged on your turnout so you always strive for bigger and better things because that's what improves your reputation and your status.

I'm lucky enough to have owned a range of flash rides because I started dealing in high-end cars. I taught Patrick the trade too. At a young age he knew cars inside and out. When he was ten he was picking out deals with me and by the time he was 14 he could spot a bargain a mile off. He was wise about all aspects of the motor trade. He could tell the make and model of a car blindfolded just by touching it. He could look over a car and identify where it had bodywork done to it, whether it had been in a crash or whether it had a new interior. He was able to tell what an engine was like just by listening to it.

He'd help me get the best deals. At that time a lot of trading was done in pubs and Patrick and I had a routine worked out. We'd spot a trader and I'd pretend to be drunk and start enquiring about cars. If there was one for sale, while the trader was describing it, Patrick would run outside, find it and have a good look over it. While I was pretending to get drunk with the person who was selling the car, Patrick would come back in and say, 'Paddy, can I have a word with you?' (He always called me Paddy.) He'd take me aside and give me the lowdown on the car and tell me what it was worth. I'd then wait until the trader had drunk a few pints with me and make an offer without even seeing it. I'd bid way below what the car was worth and usually I'd leave the pub with a car that I could sell on at a nice profit.

Patrick loved cars. When he was 17 he bought a Toyota Supra, a sports car with pop-up headlights on the bonnet. It was racing red and had a two-litre engine. He had it for less than a week before he decided he was going to sell it.

'I can't afford to run it,' he explained. 'I'm working just to pay for the petrol in it.'

I offered to help him out but Patrick was a worker and he was independent. He didn't want to be looked after; he could look after himself.

'Keep it my Par,' I told him. 'It suits you.'

He did look cool driving it around. But he was adamant and sold it at a profit.

Patrick took after me in so many ways. He had the dark skin and coal-black hair. When he was young he was thin and fit like me, only taller. He fought as well but you never knew about Patrick's fights until they were over and done with. Back then I knew my sons fought and although part of me was proud because fighting was what gypsy men did, mainly I worried and wanted to take the punches for them. It is a cruel thing for a son or a father to watch the other fight. In the boxing ring with gloves on it is fine, all my sons boxed, but going knuckle to knuckle is a different ball game completely.

Simey used to fight regularly. He was a good fighter and I saw a few of his contests. When he was a young man I watched him fight in Scotland. He went there after a late-night call to replace his brother David who had already been in a fight the day before.

David went north of the border for an organised fight and knocked his opponent clean out. He got a call from a man challenging him to a fair bare-knuckle fight and drove there from Manchester with a friend. I knew about the contest because I received a call from the fair play man for the bout – a traveller named Camella. He contacted me out of respect to let me know that David would be shown fair play. I knew Camella from old; he was a well-respected Scottish traveller. It was a mark of the man David was for him to travel there with just one friend because the crowd would have been hostile. He would have been the away team and everyone at the fight would have been rooting for their home fighter. David was the outsider and he wouldn't have been given a warm reception.

After David won his fight, the loser's brother said he wanted to fight him as well but Camella put a stop to it.

'He's had one fight, he's not having another,' he told the man.

Davey was never one to pass up an opportunity, however, and instead offered his brother up. 'I've got a brother who's big enough for you, he'll fight you,' he said.

At this point Simey knew nothing of what was being arranged for him but when Davey called him up to tell him he was fighting in Scotland the next day, Simey was happy to agree. Us Dohertys never turned down an invitation for a battle.

The following day me and Simey rounded up 40 friends and family for the trip. A convoy of us headed up the motorway and when we got to the site where the fight was taking place it was like walking into the lion's den. I had done that all my life and it meant nothing to me. It was hostile but I wasn't bothered. Simey finished off his man too and the pleasure was greater because everyone in that crowd was gutted.

A lot of money changed hands in fights where there was a tribal element. There would be a lot of side betting from people in the crowd and you could make good money if you knew a bit about the fighters because the away fighter was always the underdog. Not all fights were for money, the majority were to settle scores but with certain ones you could earn several hundred pounds.

Fighting was a career for many men. In my father's day there was a whole generation of legendary fighters. People such as Paddy Cash, Felix Rooney, Mark Baker and Henry Walton are still remembered today.

Fighting was a skill and proper fighters knew their trade with almost academic precision. The best fighters knew about anatomy and psychology. I used to know what part of the face to cut and where would bleed the most. If I was fighting and cut my opponent and then saw him wiping the blood and looking at it on his hand I knew I had the advantage because that meant he was worried about his injury. His anxiety would affect his performance. I would bleed like a tap sometimes when my eyes were cut but I never wiped or worried, I just got on with the job. I worried about the wounds after. Reading your opponent is 50 per cent of the work. I would tell an opponent when he was cut just to make him worry more. 'Do you want to get that seen to, it looks nasty,' I'd say to get inside his head and plant the seeds of doubt.

I used to love to see a black eye starting to swell because once that happened the skin got tender and just a slap could slice it. I would happily walk into a left and a right just to get that one shot at the eye because I knew it would splatter. And once the eyelid goes, he's blinded. If he has to wipe you have the opportunity to get in there. There is a skill to it, you have to think, and have a strategy. To country folk, I'm sure it sounds brutal, but your opponent was thinking the same way too, and you had to think on your feet, and fast, because any hesitation, any sign of weakness, any lack of plan, and he'd take advantage of it like a shot, and you could go down. My strength in fighting lay not just with my fists, but the fact that I could see one or two punches ahead and read my opponent. That's the way I won my fights.

The beauty of it all was that everything was fair. There were no weapons, just fists. In the old days we'd never pass up a challenge, even if it meant fighting people we'd call friends because after the fight was done, we'd be friends again. I only ever regretted one fight I had and that was one of the most talked about fights of my generation. Ironically it should never have happened because it was with my closest friend and cousin.

Johnny Coyle is a fighting man through and through and all our lives we've had nothing but love and respect for each other. We grew up together and went on holidays together with our wives. When we were younger there was an argument between the Dohertys and the Coyles. Neither of us wanted anything to do with it but we got thrown into the water, as the saying goes.

This story illustrates how easy it was to get involved in a fight. Johnny was one of the best Coyles and I was one the best Dohertys. I've long since forgotten what the argument was about but my father made the statement: 'My Patrick is the best man.' Once he said it, the challenge had thrown down. Johnny's mum, my aunt, disputed it.

And as a proud man Johnny couldn't accept that either and instead told my father: 'He's not, we're all as good as each other.'

Johnny was right, but his failure to back down gave my father a reason to challenge him.

'You fight my son, then,' he ordered.

Johnny couldn't say no and when my old man told me to fight him I couldn't say no either. To refuse would have meant disrespecting him.

The fight was arranged by my father and took place in a field in the north of England. A huge crowd of travellers gathered there to watch. I went along reluctantly because I didn't want to hurt Johnny and before we started we hugged each other. We knew that neither of us would give best to the other.

I have a habit of looking in an opponent's eyes and when I looked in Johnny's there was no badness in his face, no bitterness, no nothing. I knew that my sons, Simey and Patrick were watching from the sidelines.

For a while Johnny and I danced around each other, firing off punches to test each other out but not to hurt. Instinct took over, however, and the blows became harder. We hit each other; we hurt each other.

At one point Johnny landed a jab clean on my top lip and the force of it pushed my front teeth clean through the flesh. Blood started flowing down my chin. Johnny stopped with a concerned look on his face.

'Paddy, are you okay?' he asked.

'Hold on,' I said to him, 'let me pull my teeth out of my lip.'

I grabbed my top lip and quickly pulled it hard so the teeth popped back through it. The gaping hole that was left flapped and sprayed blood each time I puffed through it.

We carried on fighting. Neither of us had it in our hearts to beat the other but we didn't know how to back down. It was the weirdest fight I've ever had and one of the hardest.

We both took blow after blow. It was like something from a film, punch for punch, one after the other. It was proper Rocky Balboa stuff but there was one snag: there was no hatred involved, I didn't have the hunger to beat my opponent. It was a dangerous fight because it would have just gone on and on. I took his hardest and he took my hardest and I knew when he staggered under my punches and didn't go over that we would do severe harm to each other. We did. His eye was cut badly, my mouth was cut. My chin was swollen. Our ears were as black as soot. Our faces were swollen and bloody. But we carried on.

In the end, the fight was stopped. As soon as the fair play man ended it I gave Johnny a kiss and he kissed me. We both apologised and agreed to have a drink together.

After a quick clean up I met Johnny in the pub and got a pint but as soon as the liquid hit the split in my lip it burned like acid.

'There will be a lot of people who'll want us to do this again,' said Johnny. 'They'll say I beat you and others will say you beat me.'

He was telling the truth.

'I know,' I said. 'But you will never hear out of my mouth that I beat you.'

'Patrick,' he said, 'I swear on my dead brother's grave you will never hear out of my mouth that I beat you. And I will beat the first person I hear who says that.'

On the way home I made a detour to A & E to get my mouth stitched up. My Patrick was in awe. 'That's the best fight I've ever seen,' he said.

I told both him and Simey that it should never have happened. Two men as close as me and Johnny were, and still are, should never be put in a position where they have to fight each other. The fighting game can be a lonely place and you value the friends you have. It turns you into a very isolated person.

By that time I knew a lot of people and a lot of people would say they were my friend because they wanted something from me or because they were afraid of me. Davey Quinn used to be able to tell the hangers on and the users immediately and I learnt to be wary of new people in my life. Old friends and family who I had known since I was young were as valuable to me as gold because I could trust them and the bigger my reputation got, the less trusting of outsiders I became. I tried not to let the status I had attained go to my head but a lot of fighters have trouble coping with it and turn to drink or get hooked on violence. Reputation was everything but you could not let that reputation control you. You could not get too big for your boots.

Over the years I've heard people being described at the 'King of the travellers' but that's something no true traveller would ever say. Any man who calls himself a king is making a fool of himself. You can be head of your family, like my old man is king of the Doherty clan; he's the mustard, the fresh cream, the dog's bollocks and when he goes I'll take over from him because I'm the oldest son. But that hierarchy only stretched to the family. To say you are king of all travellers is hugely disrespectful. You are stating you are better than everyone else and only a sausage could make a claim like that.

14

Winning and Losing

My days went something like this. I'd get up when I wanted to go for a run. Then it would be down to business, whether that be scrap, cars or construction. I had my fingers in many pies. I was a gypsy entrepreneur. Then I'd go to the gym and train. I trained all year round to make sure I was always fit and ready to fight at the drop of a hat. For big fights, however, I would train like a pro and have plenty of time in the ring, sparring. I'd spar with the biggest and best and wouldn't wear a headguard to make sure I felt the full force of the punches. It was brutal preparation but it got me used to the weight of the impact of the punches I would feel during bare-knuckle fights. I'd call out my opponent and arrange for a fight the next morning but I wouldn't let on that I had been training six weeks before. That little ruse has mainly died out now. It was a way of gaining an advantage over your opponents. Some people saw it as cheating, I saw it as bending the rules a little but not breaking them. Today fights are arranged with plenty of notice, usually two months, so fighters both have time to train. Proper fighting men always made sure they were prepared anyway. I was a known man. My reputation spread across the UK and I was known as a fearsome fighter not just in traveller circles but also in the world of country men. I had some very powerful acquaintances and my fights brought me to the attention of the underworld.

By the nineties I was a known man in Manchester and I was mixing with the big names, some would call them gangsters but they were all men of respect; men such as Arthur Donnelly and Jimmy 'The Weed' Donnelly. I was known wherever I went and the drinks were always free in many of Manchester's finest establishments because the doors were always run by people I knew and it paid to have me as a regular because if someone was showing me hospitality, I'd help them out if help was ever needed. I had a great deal of respect for these people. Their values were the same as mine. I felt a connection, I understood their world and they understood mine. It was a world where loyalty and respect were valued above all else and were rewarded. I felt an affinity with the Manchester underworld. The kingpins were like the heads of the families I had grown up in. They loved telling stories about their escapades just like old Dudley would tell stories around the fire when I was a young, insecure kid. I'd come a long way since those days.

When I met these people I didn't care for anything so I would test the water with them and got respect in return. Truth be told, I love their company because they are old school like me. They break the rules but they play fair and they refuse to be intimidated by the younger gangsters who have no moral codes. I've seen 70-year-old men – proper old-time gangsters – go at young thugs with butcher's knives. Men like that don't ever bow down to anyone.

I'd always step in to help someone I knew if I needed too. I didn't want a Blue Peter badge, that's just the way I am.

My services were called upon at a club called Equinox that I used to frequent and is now closed. I'd gone there with my Patrick. He was 17 and I knew the man who owned the venue so we'd stopped by in the early hours one morning after the pubs had shut. Patrick could hold his drink and we were boozing away (over the years my tastes had developed and I enjoyed a good drink and a craic) when the owner asked for some assistance. A party of country lads were refusing to leave the place.

'Can you have a word with them please, Paddy?' the owner asked.

I was happy to oblige and went over to the group and asked the boys to drink up and get out.

'Who the fuck are you?' they replied.

'I'm the man who's going to knock you all out.'

'You?' said one of them, sneering into his drink. 'I'd like to see you try.'

The group guffawed. 'We'll leave when we fucking want to,' another said. 'And right now? Well, we don't want to fucking leave.'

'Get out now or be carried out by a paramedic, it's your choice,' I answered.

That did the trick and they got up and left. I carried on drinking and chatting with the landlord and Patrick when, half an hour later, we heard hammering on the door. The group had come back and they'd brought a friend with them – a big friend!

We looked at them on the CCTV monitor. I was shaking my head in bemusement. Just like always, trouble had come looking for me. They wanted a fight? Well, I was going to give them one.

'Paddy, he's a big lump of a man,' exclaimed Patrick.

'Son, watch what I do to this fool,' I answered.

We met them round the back in the car park and I agreed to fight the big fellow they'd bought along.

'Watch your daddy in action,' I laughed to Patrick with a wink as I was limbering up. I always liked to fight in front of him and was looking forward to showing him what I could do.

Just before we started, my opponent looked at me said: 'I'm an Olympic wrestler.'

I didn't have a clue what that meant. I was a proper traveller boy, I knew boxing but nothing about other fighting styles.

'What the fuck is that?' I said.

'It means I'll snap your backbone,' the man said. 'I'll break it like a twig from a tree.'

I liked fighting talk and I laughed. 'Our kid,' I replied, 'if you can break it go ahead, because I'm going to break your face.'

And with that I stepped forward and smacked him square in the face. He went down on the floor and I thought to myself, 'This will be easy'. But as he was down he grabbed me round the legs and hoisted me up in the air as if I weighed nothing. He was built like a barrel and with what seemed like no effort at all he threw me up and twisted me round so I fell down straight on my back.

The air went straight from my lungs and as I was lying on the concrete trying to get my breath back he leapt up like a jack-in-the-box and slammed his full weight on my chest. I could taste blood in my mouth and realised he was going to bust my lungs.

I got to my feet and he did it again. He ducked down, grabbed my legs and threw me down. My vision started to go. I was seeing five of him swimming around above me and I didn't know which one to hit.

Patrick could see I was in trouble and went to hit him but I called out and told him to stay out of it. He was looking at his daddy getting beat and wanted to help but I couldn't let him because my reputation would have been on the line. It was my battle and I needed to end it one way or the other.

We ended up grappling on the floor. It was a fighting style I had no experience of. The man was on top of me, beating my jaw with his elbow so I grabbed him by the hair on the top of his head and tried to bite him. As I did he tried to gouge out my eyes with his fingers. I managed to push them away and as he reached towards me again I lifted my head and clamped my mouth down on his index finger.

I bit down as hard as I could and there was no way I was letting go. As I was chomping on his digit he was banging me hard in the face with his free hand. My left eye shut and swelled within seconds. After another blow it split and blood poured out of it.

I bit down even harder and I felt the gristle in his finger joint crunching in my teeth. It was like biting through a chicken thigh. His finger went limp in my mouth, I'd bit through the joint and bone and ground my teeth together to get through the skin. The top of his finger came off in my mouth and without thinking I swallowed it. He roared in pain and I found the space to get a punch off. I beat him viciously but he had no stomach left for a fight.

'I've had enough,' he said through the pain and he was carried off cradling his hand. My eye was shut completely, and huge. My body was black with bruising. I went back in and washed myself and got clean clothes.

The wrestler must have gone to hospital where questions were asked because a little while later the police arrived and asked about the fighting. They wanted to see the CCTV of the car park but by that time all video had mysteriously been erased!

My Pat said: 'Daddy, that was a fantastic fight.'

'That wasn't fantastic, the dirty bastard was trying to blind me,' I told him.

Later, after being bandaged up, the man came back with an army of friends. I sighed when I saw them. 'What now?' I thought.

But he wanted to speak to me. 'No one's ever beaten me like that before, I want to shake your hand,' he said.

'Forget about shaking hands,' I laughed, looking at the blood-stained bandage he was wearing. And I gave him a hug to show respect.

'No one's done to me what you did,' I said. We ended up joking about me going to the loo to retrieve his finger. It was another example of how fights can make you friends not enemies.

It took a week for the swelling on my eye to go down but he would never grow another finger. I just added the scar to the long list of injuries I'd sustained. By that time I'd had my jaw broken several times and had lost count of the times my hands had been broken. My knuckle was gone, it looked like a hammer, and my face was criss-crossed with scars. But in all the battles I'd had however, I'd never lost a tooth and to this day all my teeth are my own.

Around the same time as my fighting reputation was reaching its peak Roseanne fell pregnant again. We greeted the news with mixed feelings. There was the joy that we were blessed with another child but the apprehension that the baby Roseanne carried could have Fraser syndrome. It had been three years since Helen died and the memory of the tragedy was still fresh in our minds.

Roseanne was very anxious and no matter how hard I tried to reassure her, she could not relax. Initially the scan held a massive surprise – it was twins. We were delighted. Perhaps it was God's way of replacing the two babies who had died.

The hospital kept a close eye on the babies all the way through. For most couples it is a wonderful time when you plan for your new child but for us it was a nightmare. If the babies didn't move for a few hours we would fear the worst and we just wanted those nine months out the way and for the twins to be born.

It seemed like we had almost made it too. But at 38 weeks Roseanne went to a routine antenatal appointment and was given devastating news. One of the babies had died.

Roseanne was distraught; she was carrying one live and one dead child inside her. The appointment was on a Tuesday and the doctors explained that they would perform a Caesarean section the following Tuesday to deliver the healthy child.

Call it female intuition but Roseanne had an awful feeling and refused to wait that long. She believed that the surviving twin was also sick and would not survive a week.

She was hysterical.

'Don't lie to me,' she told the doctor. 'If you send me home I'm going to kill myself because I know by this time next week the second child will be dead. I might as well die now because I can't bear another two dead babies. I can't take any more.'

That made them listen and three days later Roseanne went to have the operation. The twins were a boy and a girl. The girl, who we named Mary Bridget, was dead. The boy, Martin Tom, was alive but made no sound at all and was very weak.

He was taken away and put into a special care baby unit where it was discovered he had a severe infection. He had picked it up from his sister. If he had been left for much longer he would have died.

Martin Tom was weak and it took many days before he started to respond to the medication he was given. He was so ill he didn't cry for five weeks after he was born. It was hard to be happy because his birth was tinged with tragedy and it was hard to grieve for Mary Bridget because Martin Tom was ill and we needed to be strong for him. But thanks to what Roseanne did and her insistence that the doctors took action, he survived.

Physical pain means nothing to me. I can take on any man in the land and he can beat me till I'm reeling, but I'll still come back fighting. I won't give best to anyone. But emotional pain – that's something different. Seeing my children suffering, seeing my woman in tears because another baby had entered this world only to be taken by the angels, well, that floored me in a way no fists ever could. I had a reputation for being a Doherty; a hard man, a fighting man. But when it came to my woman and my children, I was all heart. No matter what anyone tells you, losing your children, even the ones you know for just a few short moments, is something you never get over.

15

Work, Fight and Play

I never knew what defeat felt like. I never allowed myself to be beaten and I would die before I gave best to another man. The closest my pride came to being taken from me happened on a day I wasn't due to be fighting.

To understand the story you need to understand the history. There is a fighting family called the Rooneys. Several years before the fight in question Ned Rooney gave a cousin of mine a hiding, so afterwards I tried to arrange a fight with Ned. However, he was locked up at the time so we agreed to have the fight when he was released. But when he did get out the fight was squashed (called off, as country folk would say) because Ned wasn't allowed to fight. I think it was something to do with his bail conditions and understandably he didn't want to go back inside. So we left it there, no problems, no arguments. Three years later, Ned's brother Dan was fighting Mullingar's Joe Joyce in Manchester. Dan was rated one of the best Rooney men so it was a big affair. I wanted to watch and headed along to the pub where fighters and spectators had arranged to meet. The building is now an insurance office. I went along with Roseanne and had a few drinks. I was relaxing and looking forward to a good fight on a Saturday afternoon, the way many men look forward to watching a game of football. I was there to support Joe and the pub was on the Rooneys' home turf so it was full of them and their supporters. The atmosphere was slightly prickly but nothing I couldn't handle. While I was at the bar Ned came in. He saw me and walked over.

'I'm going to ask you a question,' he said, pointing his finger at me like a child. 'Are you as good a man as they say? Are you good enough to fight me?'

I turned to face him. When talk got to fighting a switch went on in my head. I was programmed for violence. I didn't know how to say no and in my heart of hearts I believed I could beat any man. To decline an offer of a fight was to show weakness and fighting travellers never showed weakness. Even if he was three foot taller than me and built like a brick shithouse I would have to accept an invitation to fight. 'No I'm a better man,' I said.

'Let's go outside the door now then,' he offered.

And that was that. The fight was on. It was the first time Roseanne had been at what I would class as a proper fight. The spur of the moment pub fights with country folk she had witnessed before didn't count. This was going to be a proper fight with one of the thoroughbreds of gypsy fighters. There was no planning for this one and I couldn't help that she was there. Usually no women are allowed at fights. It's man's stuff. We don't want our women distracting us and fussing over us. Roseanne didn't have a say in the matter. I'm sure if it was up to her she would have had me walk away but she knew better than to argue or try to persuade me not to accept a challenge. I'm sure she hated it. But no matter how much I loved and cared for her, this was something I had to do.

We went out into an alley at the side of the pub and the place emptied out as everyone came out to watch. The alleyway was only a few feet wide so there wasn't much room to move around and Ned was a big man. But I found the space and moved in out of his reach. I scored the first big punch, which rocked his head back and sent him to the ground. I'm going to show off now, I thought to myself.

'Get up,' I ordered, and after another few punches he went down again.

When he got up the second time the crowd shifted. Sensing blood they closed in and suddenly I realised I was in close quarters with him and didn't have the space to move around. The goalposts had moved. He was too heavy for me, he was like a tank. *Bam!* He hit me and I slid down the wall. As I slid he hit me under the chin with an uppercut and lifted me back up. He did it repeatedly and I couldn't move out of range. I was up and down the wall like a yo-yo. He made me feel like I was nothing. I could hear Roseanne crying and screaming in the crowd.

'Shut up woman,' I called out. And then I felt my rib go. The wind was punched out of me and I was getting battered around badly. I managed to catch him and I could see him wobble but as I tried to open some distance between us he grabbed me and turned me round again and put my back against the wall. The onslaught continued until finally I felt myself going down. As I did something very lucky happened. Ned hit me on the ground.

'Hold on,' I called out. 'I'm not getting fair play here. I'm down.'

Those were the rules in them days, no hitting when a man was down.

The crowd, which had been jeering for my blood, went quiet. I was right, according to the rules Ned had transgressed.

I could see the frustration on his face.

'You give best to me,' he said.

'No way,' I said.

'Then carry the fight on,' he ordered.

'I'm not fighting you until I get someone to show fair play,' I told him. I was well within my rights after his mistake. The rest of the travellers knew that was the case, the fight was fairly stopped on a technicality and Ned had to agree to fight me at another time and venue.

I wish I could say that was the end of it but the episode ate up my heart. It bore its way into my soul. The idea that there was a man out there who could claim to have beaten me drove me half insane. I couldn't service my woman, I went to bed with Ned in my head and woke up with him still there. I couldn't work and all I could think about was fighting him again. Matters were made worse because Ned had gone off travelling and I didn't know where to find him.

About six months later I had a lucky break. I discovered that there was a big wedding taking place in Manchester at the Britannia Hotel and that Ned Rooney was going to be there. On the afternoon of the wedding I headed into town to challenge my nemesis.

Roseanne must have known something was up by the look in my eye. 'Where are you going?' she asked.

I looked at her grimly and didn't say a word.

'Paddy, tell me, where are you going?' she pressed.

'I'm going to find Ned Rooney and I'm going to beat the shit out of him,' I replied.

Her lovely face went pale. 'Paddy, I know that this has been eating away at you, but why can't you let this go?'

'Woman, I can't,' I answered. 'I won't be able to hold my head up knowing that Ned Rooney could have got the best of me. I have to do this. I have to lay the ghost of this fight to rest.'

Roseanne knew she couldn't talk me out of it. I left the trailer and went on my way to find Ned Rooney.

At the hotel there were hundreds of guests; all Rooneys. I walked in and the crowd parted like the Red Sea. Everyone knew me and they knew why I was there. I walked to the bar and as I did a man stood in my way. 'You're Paddy Doherty, aren't you? Why would you think you can best Ned, he beat you already.'

'No,' I answered. 'I'm here to see Ned and I'm going to get the best of him today.'

As we were squaring up Ned came over. 'Hello Paddy, how are you?' he asked, nice as pie.

I shook his hand.

Ned had nothing to prove, I was the one who had to prove myself because I took a hiding. He could afford to be charming. But I didn't have time for pleasantries.

'Listen, Ned, I'm here to fight you,' I said.

He laughed, which pissed me off even more. 'I've been drinking all day so I won't fight you now. But I tell you what I'll do. I'll fight you in the morning,' he said.

'I'll fight you anywhere in the world, anytime,' I answered.

Then Dan came over and slapped me on the shoulder. 'Fair play to you coming here and showing some front,' he said.

I gave Ned the address of a field where we could fight and we arranged to meet there the following morning. As I walked out Ned called to me: 'Hey, Patrick! Make sure you turn up in the morning for your beating because I want to go to work straight after.' He made sure the whole room heard it, just to be cocky.

Next morning I got up but I wasn't going to give Ned the satisfaction of ordering me around and I didn't go to meet him until late in the afternoon, just to keep him waiting. It was a big affair. My father was there with my brothers Hughie, Johnny and Simey and my cousin Johnny Coyle. There were hundreds of people.

Ned smiled when he saw me. 'So you decided to come then,' he said.

'Sorry I'm late, Ned, I was out looking for work,' I told him. I wanted him to know that's how bothered I was. It was a winter's day but we both stripped off to the waist and squared up.

The fight began. *Bang bang!* Ned caught me with a combination and I went down. The man could hit like a jackhammer. I got up and shook my head.

'Nice punch, Ned,' I said.

'That's nothing compared to what I'm going to do to you,' he replied. We went at it again and the next time I caught Ned and he went down.

I said to him: 'That's nothing, I'm going to put you in hospital.' We were having a bit of banter.

It went on and on, blow for blow. It was brutal. I knew there was blood coming out of me but I didn't know from where. It was all over my face like a glistening mask. At one point we were under a lorry scuffling and when it started to get dark we took a break while a group of travellers made a circle with their cars and turned the lights on so we had a makeshift floodlit ring.

I could see his face properly in the headlights and it was a mess. He was a bloody pulp. I didn't realise it at the time but I was just as bad.

Dan tried to intervene.

'There is no shame in anyone giving best here,' he said. He could see what we knew in our hearts. That both of us would die before we gave in. 'You are two great men,' he added.

But neither of us wanted to end it. We fought so heavily we fell on each other. After about 40 minutes we were hitting each other but there was nothing left in our punches. Still we carried on. My face was getting bigger and bigger. I could feel it inflate as if it was a balloon and someone was blowing it up. It was a ruthless fight. There was nothing in us yet we wanted to kill each other and we probably would have.

To stop such a tragedy my father and Dan stepped in and called a halt.

I argued against the decision. 'You can't, because there's no best,' I mumbled through swollen lips.

'I wouldn't give best to you, I'd sooner die,' Ned said to me. Fair play to this man, I thought. I wanted to destroy him but I admired him.

'Listen,' he said, 'Let's forget it now.'

He was right; we would have ended up killing each other. We shook hands and then his wife came out with a dish of water and a towel for me to wash the blood off my face. I thought it was the loveliest thing. There were no hard feelings at all. In fact, that fight brought us together and we became good friends, so much so that years later I went to his son's wedding. When we get drunk we have a laugh about how we came to within a whisker of killing each other.

It wasn't all work and fighting of course. I knew how to enjoy myself and the best friend I had was my Patrick. As he got to his late teens we weren't like father and son, we were like brothers. We did everything together. There wasn't a huge age gap between us, 19 years, and we would go to raves together in a big abandoned factory in Wigan in the late nineties.

Patrick was great company. He would light up a room when he walked in it. One of our regular haunts was a place called Sportsbar in Deansgate in Manchester. At the time it was the club to go to, and most weekends you'd find me and my Par in there. Roseanne always believed he didn't drink but Patrick could drink a man under the table, even in his late teens. Then he'd get up in the morning and train. He was good-looking, tall and the women flocked to him. He had grown into a great man, he was everything I wanted him to be. He was going steady with a traveller girl called Katrina who lived in London. He loved her and she loved him.

Patrick was always betting me. A few days before his 18th birthday he set me a challenge. We were talking about running and Patrick turned to me and said: 'I bet you couldn't run a marathon.'

I laughed. 'I bet I could,' I said.

'A hundred says you can't,' he challenged.

I couldn't turn him down and I shook his hand on it. 'I'll do it next year,' I said.

A few weeks before his 18th birthday I arranged a party for him in Sportsbar. Loads of family and friends turned up and I put a nice few quid behind the bar to make sure everyone enjoyed themselves.

I'm not ashamed of this, in fact I'm proud, on that night, me and a couple of other men I was with who should have also known better dropped Es. It was the nineties, everyone was popping pills like crazy. Raves were massive and I lived in Manchester, right in the middle of the rave scene. Taking those pills chilled me out, meant that I wasn't sizing up every man in the bar to see whether he wanted to have a go or not.

We were in the bar early and by the time Patrick came in I was tripping off my head. It was a hilarious night. I tried to be sensible and to make sure everything went to plan but I couldn't. Patrick grabbed the mic and started singing the Engelbert Humperdink song 'Quando, Quando, Quando'. The DJ got fed up with him and wanted to get on with his set and the owner begged me to get my son off the stage but all I could do was laugh.

'Get down, Patrick,' I shouted, but he looked in my eyes, which were as wide as dinner plates and he knew I was out of my tree. He laughed. Roseanne didn't have a clue.

When you take those Es you love everyone. If a man came up to me with a knife at that point I would have given him a hug. I felt amazing. I was so used to showing the hard side of myself, of being the hard man and looking for trouble it was a novelty to relax and be myself. Patrick realised this and realised that his dad was chilled out and worked out a little scheme.

He sidled up to me later in the night.

'Paddy, can I borrow the Range Rover for a couple of days?' he asked sweetly. 'I want to go to London and see my woman.'

I had a lovely Range Rover that I had bought. It was top of the range and fully loaded with extras. It was my pride and joy.

'What am I going to drive?' I asked.

'My van,' he said. He had a big dirty van.

I scoffed but he begged and he gave me a hug and a kiss and eventually got round me.

'Go one then,' I gave in. 'That'll do, take that jeep whenever you want to.' He knew he'd only get the chance while the Ecstasy was in me and the minute I agreed he took the keys and he was gone.

I forgot all about it and enjoyed the rest of the night. I came down later and went looking for Patrick, only to realise he had gone and my car had gone. I slowly realised what I'd allowed him to do. The next morning I was mad. He'd taken the piss. I had to confess to Roseanne what he'd done.

'Spinx took my fucking Range Rover to London,' I said (we called him Spinx because when he was young and his front milk teeth fell out he looked like the boxer Leon Spinks – the name stuck even when his adult teeth grew through). I told her he took advantage of me when I was drunk, I couldn't tell her I was popping disco biscuits. Roseanne was protective of Patrick like any mother and didn't like the thought of him driving around in a big powerful car. She blamed me.

'I'll kill him when he gets back,' I said.

'Leave the child alone,' she ordered.

Patrick came back several days later in the evening and he was all over me in a way he wasn't usually, offering to make me tea and being particularly nice. I knew there was something wrong. The next morning I got up and saw a slick of oil underneath the Range Rover.

'What the fuck have you done to the car, Patrick?' I accused.

He looked sheepish. 'I've done nothing,' he swore.

I knew he was a maniac driver. 'How fast were you going?' I said.

He told me he stuck to the speed limit all the way there and back. I checked the engine for oil and it was bone dry. I started the motor and it made a loud knocking noise. Patrick had blown up the engine.

'You've got some work to help me with,' I said.

We filled the engine with thick JCB oil to dull the knocking sound and washed the car down, vacuumed the inside and polished it. It was metallic green and a fine vehicle. It looked as good as new when we'd finished.

'You better pray I get my money back for this,' I warned him, but I could never stay mad at Pat for long.

We took it in the auction together. The car was sold as seen. There were no comebacks and the buyers, who were usually traders anyway, knew the risks when they started bidding. We did make the money back. Little did I know that it was the last motor we would ever sell together.

16

19 July 1996

Some days remain etched on your mind like a tattoo. You remember all the details from beginning to end with such clarity that you can relive them at will. 19 July 1996 is one of those days. The events are branded on my heart and in my head. A bullet couldn't erase them. I return to that day often and each time I do my heart breaks afresh. But no matter how painful, memories of that day will never fade. I can never forget.

It was a Friday. The Euro '96 football championships were on and a month before, on Patrick's 18th birthday, the IRA had bombed Manchester city centre. The town was still in shock. The bomb had decimated the Arndale Centre. I had bought Patrick a beautiful gold pair of boxing gloves on a heavy gold belcher chain. I was supposed to pick it up from the jewellers in town on the day of his birthday, but because of the bomb I hadn't been able to get into the city centre. So that Friday morning I drove in to collect it. I weighed the gift up in my hand. It was a good lump of gold.

Meanwhile, Patrick was with his brothers in the other trailer. It had been a baking July and that day was an absolute scorcher, so I decided early that we were going to have a family outing.

Mr Par was officially a man now, and a fine man at that, but he had grown up long before. One of his best friends was his cousin David – Martin and Teresa's son. The two of them made Martin and me proud. They too were fighters but we never heard about their battles because they didn't want to bother us. They were proper men. But, adulthood didn't stop Par having fun with his younger brothers and sisters and when I suggested a trip to the canal where I went swimming as a kid, he was the first to agree.

We headed off before lunch. There was me, Patrick, Simey, David, Margaret and Johnny. Martin Tom was still a toddler so he stayed home with his mammy. All the kids looked up to Patrick and he took care of them and told them what to do when he needed to.

Patrick was wearing a pair of shorts and the seam had ripped on them, I was laughing and winding him up, telling him that he ought to be careful in case he fell out of them.

'Holy fuck,' I said. 'You want to cover that thing up. It'll put a smile on a few faces.'

We stayed in the canal for hours. It reminded me of my childhood. The canal was always the place I went to get away from the bullies and the stresses of life. It was my escape and a place where I could be a child for a few hours. I watched my children play and smiled to myself; none of us had a care in the world that afternoon.

We stayed there for most of the day and left late to get some food. A few days before, I bought a car from Blondie Simey and

I asked Patrick to go and pick it up. I gave him the money and he got a lift there and returned an hour later with the car.

He had £50 change to give me.

'Paddy,' he said sweetly – I knew what was coming next. 'I want to go out tonight to a rave, can you loan me £40?'

I smiled to myself, he didn't miss a trick. He knew I had a spare £50.

'Here, keep the 50,' I said, and handed him the money. Good luck to him, I thought, go and enjoy yourself. He had arranged to go with David and one of his friends and he walked off to find them.

'Par,' I called after him. 'I've got something else for you.'

He turned round and walked back, a quizzical look in his eyes. 'What is it Paddy?'

I reached into my pocket and pulled out the jewellery box that contained the boxing gloves.

'Happy birthday my son,' I said.

Patrick took it excitedly. He'd loved jewellery all his life. When he was a baby I bought him a chain with an ounce bar of gold on it. When we put it on him he could hardly lift his head up.

His eyes glinted when he held out the gloves in front of him. 'I don't know what to say Paddy. It's beautiful,' he said, grinning like a Cheshire cat.

'Come here,' I beckoned. I pulled him closer, took the chain off him and fixed it round the back of his neck.

'Be lucky my Par,' I said and kissed his cheek.

If I'd have known that was the last time I would ever see him alive I would have made that parting last for ever and told him how much I loved him.

It only seemed like he'd been gone for a few minutes when I got the call. When I picked up the phone I knew something terrible had happened. It sounds clichéd but it's the truth. I don't know why; instinct maybe, but I had a feeling of deep unease.

'Paddy, it's Dar,' the voice on the other end of the line was one of my nephews. 'I think your Patrick is dead…'

The words hung in the air. I blinked. I didn't understand.

'You're wrong, he only left ten minutes ago,' I said.

'There's been an accident,' Dar continued. 'The boys were in a car. I'm here now, it's a bad crash Paddy. Patrick is dead.'

He told me where it was, it was just a few minutes away on the East Lancs Road, near the site Roseanne and I first moved on to after we married. The car was still there, the emergency services were at the scene. I got in my car and drove to my son, my heart was racing as adrenaline surged through me. Roseanne was at her sister's house nearby and I told Margaret who was at home to call her mother and tell her what had happened.

Patrick was in the car with Martin's son, David and a friend called Andrew. The scene when I arrived was carnage. The car they were in had gone underneath a juggernaut. I could see it and I could see their car wedged underneath but the road was taped off and I couldn't get to the wreckage. It seemed like there were hundreds of police, ambulance and fire crews there.

I got out and ran to the accident. A policeman stopped me. 'You can't go there sir,' he said.

The panic was bursting through me. 'My son's in that car,' I said. 'I need to see him.'

The man took me aside and tried to calm me. He told me that there were two people in the car and that the fire crews were cutting through it to try and get them out. I knew there were three boys in the car.

I said: 'Listen, jackass, I know my son is in there. I want to see him.'

Before he could answer I heard a shout.

'There's another body in there... wait, he's alive.'

My heart leapt. I knew instinctively it was my Patrick. I started shouting and screaming to him. There were tears flowing down my face.

'Listen to me, my Patrick,' I called out. 'You are a Doherty, like your daddy, fight this one. You've fought all your life, fight now, my son, don't give up. You are a man's man. Fight like you've never fought before.'

I was being restrained by then and I could see them cutting the roof off the car. Andrew and David had been in the front seats and had taken the full force of the impact. They died instantly. God bless them, their faces took the impact, they had no faces left. Patrick managed to duck down in the rear footwell just in time. He was crushed in a tiny space.

I kept calling and crying. 'Your daddy's here, Par.' I'd never said the word 'daddy' to him, I was always Paddy to him or the old man.

The police explained that I needed to let the firemen do their work and that it would be better if I waited in the ambulance.

They could see I was in shock and they helped me into the back of one of the ambulances. There was a man in there with me. He had a blanket wrapped round him and he was shaking despite the heat of the evening. His eyes were red-rimmed. He was the driver of the juggernaut.

You'd imagine I would go about killing this man but I could feel his suffering.

'It wasn't my fault,' he kept saying.

I sat next to him and I put my arm around him. We both sobbed.

'Sir,' he said, 'I was driving along and they hit me. There was nothing I could do.'

He was so traumatised and my heart bled for him. I sat in that ambulance for what seemed like an eternity comforting the man who drove the vehicle that had killed my nephew and my cousin. He was a wreck. I tried to calm him down. I gave the man a kiss. I was heartbroken but I knew at that point he was worse than me. He was eaten up by pain. At that moment I didn't know that Patrick was going to die but it wouldn't have made a difference if I had. I looked at this man, I looked into his eyes and could see that he would never get over what had just happened.

I was waiting for about half an hour when a policeman came in and told me that Patrick had been taken from the car and was on the way to hospital. They were taking me there too. We followed the ambulance and as we pulled up outside A & E Patrick was being wheeled inside.

I shouted to him again. 'Fight! Fight my son!'

By this time Roseanne was there and we went up to the emergency room. Word spreads quickly and other travellers had begun to arrive who were related to Andrew and David.

'Where's our Martin?' I said to Roseanne. 'I hope Davey's okay.' I was confused and in shock by that time and I had forgotten that Davey and Andrew were dead.

They took Patrick into the operating theatre. Someone came and told us that he had sustained internal injuries and that he was bleeding heavily. They were operating to try to stem the flow of blood inside him.

We waited in there for 90 minutes while a few yards away the life was draining from my son. Each of those minutes felt like a year. I was lost in my head, swaying between hope and despair. Roseanne was in her own world of pain, sobbing and screaming.

Eventually a doctor came in the room.

'Who are the parents of the lad with the gold bracelet and the boxing glove on it?' he asked softly.

I stood bolt upright from my seat.

'He's mine,' I said. 'I own him. The black-haired boy, yep he's mine.' They asked my name. I was shouting. 'Let me see him.'

Roseanne told me to quiet down and I snapped.

'Shut up, woman,' I told her.

'Mr Doherty, we have some bad news,' the man said. 'We've lost your son.'

The words didn't register.

'What do you mean "we've lost him"?' I said. 'He's in there.'

The doctor repeated himself.

I didn't know what he meant. That earth-shattering fact he was trying to tell me wouldn't go into my head, I wouldn't let it. I told the doctor to go back in the room and look, I grabbed him and said, 'Come with me and I'll bring you to him.' He fixed me with a look that stopped me in my tracks.

'Mr Doherty, your son has died,' he said firmly.

It was as if all the tumblers in a lock in my head had clicked into place and the realisation of what had happened suddenly hit me harder than the hardest punch I could ever take. The noise that came out of me wasn't human, it was made of heartbreak and torment. Roseanne was screaming, beating her chest and pulling at her hair.

Everyone else in the room was silent; transfixed by the gruesome spectacle of two people caught in time as their world collapsed around them. Eventually, through my tears and sobs, I asked to go and see Patrick. We were led to the room and he was lying there covered in a sheet. There wasn't a scratch on his face. Not a hair out of place. He was pale, which made his black hair even darker. He looked peaceful, like he was asleep. Roseanne was beating herself; she screamed his name and cradled his head.

I stood behind her and stared. I was transfixed. Patrick was beautiful; he looked like he was in no pain. He didn't look like he was dead. He looked pure. He looked like he did when he left me, so I couldn't understand how he could be dead.

'This isn't happening', I said to myself, 'he was only with me swimming a few hours before.'

Roseanne was shaking him. 'Patrick, wake up for your mummy,' she was begging.

I was frozen there for ages trying to put order to my thoughts and to push down the waves of panicked grief that were threatening to overwhelm me. I looked down at his body and saw that his leg was sticking out from under the covers that the doctors had put over him. His ankle was broken and the bone had come out through his skin. There was blood dripping from the wound.

A thought began to formulate in my mind. I knew Patrick was dead and he was going to be buried. After he was put in the ground I would never own him again. He wouldn't be mine any more. He would belong to God. I wouldn't have any of him left.

I've thought many times about what I did in that room next and sometimes I think maybe it had something to do with my beliefs. Mass had been a big part of my life, taking the blood and the body of Christ. People might think it was disgusting but it wasn't for me. My child was pure and I was absolutely bereft. While Roseanne cradled Patrick's head, I went down and I kissed his feet. I looked at his wound and at the flesh and the blood dripping out of it. I kissed his wound and as I was kissing it I let the blood and a small piece of his flesh go in my mouth. It made me feel better. I knew that when he was buried he would live on inside me. He was my flesh and blood and he would become my flesh and blood again. He would live on inside me. I really believed that.

A male nurse came in the room. 'You have to come out the room for a while now,' he said gently.

'It'll take more than you to get me out of here,' I growled.

He said: 'Just give us one minute and then you can come back.'

So I went out the room with Roseanne and when we walked back in Roseanne went back to the head of the bed to stroke Patrick's face and I went to the bottom. Roseanne said she wanted a lock of his hair so we carefully cut some off. Later I got it made into a gold locket with PD etched on it. It is one of the most precious things we own.

We were left in the room for an hour before they took Patrick away to the mortuary. We couldn't leave the hospital. I couldn't leave while my son was still there. It was as if there was a bond keeping me tied to him and if I broke that bond it would mean that he was gone. There were many travellers there that night. Friends and family and half of them I can't even remember. I was in a daze. They came to honour the dead and to offer support. They filled the waiting rooms and the car park.

At one point during the night I saw Martin again. I recognised in him the haunted despair I was feeling. 'My David died,' he kept saying.

Later we were allowed to go and see our sons together in the mortuary. The three boys were laid out in a room on three cold slabs. Andrew and David were in a bad way, but there wasn't a hair on Patrick's head out of place. It was a scene of horror, there were three wasted lives cut short just when they should have been starting their adult lives and looking forward to all the opportunities that lay ahead. When I saw David and Andrew I said, 'Thank you, my God, you took my son but you kept his looks.' The accident had erased their features. As much as I was in pain, I couldn't fathom what Martin felt or Andrew's parents because I could recognise my child.

I still can't find words to explain the depth of pain I felt. No matter what I think of, it never seems enough. Me and Roseanne were in our own worlds then. There was no cuddling or comforting, neither of us could see past our own grief.

I don't know what time we left or who took us home in the end. The other children needed to be told and we needed to be together as a family, even though there was a huge part of us missing. I left the hospital half the man I was when I got there. A huge part of me had been ripped away and what was left was a gaping dark empty wound. I could only think of my own loss. All my hopes and dreams died that night and I just wanted the waves of grief that swept over me to carry me away. I just wanted to be with my Patrick.

Back home, Roseanne and I were so traumatised all we could do was retch, moan and weep. We didn't talk to each other; we weren't capable of coherent speech. At some point in the early hours a doctor came and gave us both tranquillisers. Roseanne wanted to leave this world and so did I. I swallowed a handful. Eventually the dark came and took me. I never wanted to wake up.

17

Sins of the Father

It was shocking just how quickly life fell apart. Patrick was the centre of my world and without him there was nothing to hold all the parts together. In the days after his death I was a zombie. I was overcome with grief and needed help just to function. I couldn't get up, I couldn't focus. I was useless. The doctor was called out because of the state I was in and I was prescribed tranquillisers. I swallowed them as if they were sweets in a vain effort to dull the world around me. I wanted to escape from my life and from how I felt. I couldn't handle the weight of the grief. I couldn't accept he had gone.

God forgive me but when I was away from the other children I kept crying: 'He can't go, take all my children but he can't go. I can't live without him.'

I can't explain in words the extent of how I felt because there are not words strong enough to describe it. I was burning in hell. I wouldn't wish those feelings on anyone; not even my worst enemy. It wasn't simply pain; my heart was being slowly ripped out of me, day after day. It was so much torture. They say time heals but even then I knew it wouldn't. If I survived, I knew I would never get over what had happened and that ultimately it would change the person I was. The loss would become part of who I was.

Not long before Patrick died we sold the Range Rover he wrecked and it made around £10,000. That was the money I used to bury my son. It paid for the funeral and for the casket.

The funeral was a week after he died and was the biggest I had ever seen and even though I was in the middle of it, I barely knew I was there. The three boys who died in the accident were all buried together in Gorton. Patrick was buried in what was now the family plot alongside his sisters. There were thousands of people there; they were standing on the roofs of vans and in the trees. You couldn't get into the cemetery. All my people were there – the Dohertys, the Wards – all my brother Martin's people were there and all Andrew's people were there. It seemed that almost every traveller in Great Britain and Ireland came that day. But I felt alone and isolated. I was taking tranquillisers by the handful just to dull the terrifying grief I felt. It was overbearing. The only person I wanted to be with was buried under the earth.

That morning I didn't want to be around anyone and I got in my car and drove. I was in a daze; I don't even know where I went. The sense of motion soothed me. The world blurred as it sped past the windows of my Mercedes, faster and faster. I wanted to escape. I kept thinking how I just had to yank the steering wheel to one side and I'd send the car into a tree. I was hurtling towards a dark place in my mind. I wanted to end it all. But the survival instinct that had kept me alive and fighting all my life was too strong to override.

Back at home in the trailer Roseanne was in her own world of hurt. She had closed herself off to the rest of the world as had I. She didn't want to be around anyone either. We were drifting further and further apart. We were hardly speaking. I'm a traveller man and we don't do feeling and thoughts. We keep our emotions buried, we don't share. And so at a time when I could have been a support for my wife and she could have been a support for me, we grew apart.

We came together at the funeral, at our son's graveside. We looked at each other, both of us out of our heads with grief and tranquillisers. We were lost souls. It was unheard of for traveller men to show affection in public. I truly wanted to give her some words of comfort. I was the only man on the planet who knew how much she was suffering. But there was no comfort there. At that moment all I yearned for was to go home, crawl into bed and to lay my head on her chest and go to sleep.

The wake was a huge affair. The accident and details of how big the funeral would be had already been in the newspapers and venues were worried about the prospect of hosting so many travellers. They literally swarmed to the city. In the end it took the intervention of my Manchester friends to help organise things. Jimmy The Weed's sons, Dominic and Tony Donnelly, arranged a venue and organised everything along with a man called Steve Bailer. They never came to me once, they just did it all.

When they lowered his casket into the hole I stood at the lip of the grave and watched as the bronze box slowly inched into the earth. The whole place was silent except for the sound of weeping. My brothers and me all caved in. I hope we never have to do that again because it broke our hearts. Roseanne was distraught.

'No, my Patrick,' she was crying, 'you can't leave us.'

I was wearing a black suit and shirt and I took my tie off and threw it into the grave on top of the coffin. Then I took a shovel from the pile of earth next to the grave and I started to fill my son's grave in. All you could hear was the sound of me roaring and of earth hitting the lid of the casket. I was drowning in sweat and tears, I didn't care. It's an awful thing to put dirt on top of your child.

I fell to my knees and my old fella stepped forward. 'Come on son, hold your head up,' he said.

I raised my face to his. My eyes were dead, bloodshot and empty. 'I have no heart, I have nothing,' I croaked. I was wretched. I was finished.

I saw his eyes fill up as he looked down at me and he's not an emotional man, he doesn't do that. He knew how fucked up I was. That night Roseanne got into bed with me and put her head on my chest. We went to sleep like two children. We just wanted the world to go away.

A few days later my father tried to pull me out of my misery again. 'You're broke now Patrick,' he said. 'Everyone wants to see the way you are now.' It was his way of helping me. He was trying to get through to my fighting spirit, to shake it up and to reawaken it. You see, although the travelling community is close and we all come together at times of need there is also a lot of jealousy and envy. There were plenty of people who would have relished seeing me ruin myself. The old man even gave me a mare as a present. I used to go for drives with her. I could hitch her up to a trap and head out on the road and forget about my pain for a while.

In the days and weeks that followed the funeral I returned to the grave again and again. I wanted to be near my son. In the sleepless nights when the grief threatened to overrun me I would go to the only place I felt comfort. I'd turn up sometimes at 3 a.m. and climb the gates so I could sit there for hours and hours. Sometimes the rain would be teeming out of the heavens and I would sit there on the grave. When I was a kid I used to be frightened of cemeteries. I found them spooky, but Gorton was the only place I could find a little bit of peace for my tortured heart. I missed Patrick so much; I was pining for him.

I was too wrapped up in my own pain to realise that everyone else was suffering too. Roseanne went through worse than I did because she had been grieving in the two years before Patrick died. In that time she had lost her father, her mother and her brother. She was in a world of hurt too but rather than comfort her and stay with her I drifted off into my own world. I went looking for things to deaden the pain that was eating away at me. Before Patrick died I used to take an Ecstasy tablet every so often. It was fun, it was a laugh, and it was something I could take or leave. But after he left us I looked for ways to dull my senses and I took to drugs. I'm ashamed to say I took more Ecstasy and even cocaine. They were an escape. I started to drink heavily and I would go off for days on end, leaving my family to cope without me. I'm ashamed of the way I behaved now and if I could take back the hurt I gave people then I would but I was delirious with loss. I could think of nothing but Patrick.

All my life I had assumed I could deal with pain. Physical punishment meant nothing to me; it was like water off a duck's back. But even the combined pain of all the beatings and all the punches I had ever taken would be like the touch of a feather compared to what I felt.

Five months after Patrick died we went to my father's for the first Christmas without him. The old man was living in Cardiff at the time and we took the children. We were like refugees, the whole lot of us slept in one bed because we wanted to be together. All Roseanne and me did was cry. We tried hard not to show our pain in front of the children but it was so hard because that time of year is all about family. All the adverts on TV were about happy families. Everywhere we looked we were being reminded of our loss.

We used to go into the bedroom to cry but the children knew how much in pain we were in and they would cry too. Children are resilient, they don't have the kind of prolonged grief adults have, they have sad moments, then the next minute they go off and play. Although it was lovely that we were all there together I couldn't help thinking that we shouldn't have been celebrating without Par. If I laughed I felt guilty and ashamed for allowing myself to be distracted from my grief. That went on for a long, long time. I always had a sour face but I couldn't help it. Beforehand I loved jeering and blackguarding, it was natural to me, a way of life, but afterwards that had gone. I cared for nothing. I wouldn't have cared if I went to live in a tent. I used to love my cars and my turnout but none of that meant anything any more. I even stopped caring how I dressed.

Soon after the accident I got an offer to move away from Manchester completely. Everywhere I went in the city there were reminders of Patrick, and so Roseanne and I decided that it would be wise to move away to try and give ourselves some space to grieve. Because of my standing within the traveller community I had been given the option of running a traveller site in Scunthorpe. The site I was invited onto was a transit site that was used by families while they waited for permanent pitches or accommodation. It was a no-go area and the people on it were being hounded by local country men and I was asked to go and look after them and manage the site. I had done the same at a previous camp in Stockport and was known to councils as a man who could turn things around. Like any walk of life there are certain rules people need to obey on council-run sites, there is rent to pay and utility bills to cover. The councils who ran the sites needed someone they could trust and someone the travellers respected to make sure the sites ran smoothly. I had always mixed with country people and understood their ways and so I guess I was an automatic choice.

If truth be told, I enjoyed the challenge. I knew wherever I went there was likely to be trouble and I never told Roseanne that I was being employed to deal with it. When I walked on the site in Scunthorpe the people there knew who I was and they knew I was being brought in to keep order. They loved it because they knew they were safe. We had a trailer right by the entrance of the site so anyone who came in had to get past me first.

I did my homework before I moved. I knew there was a local gangster who was coming on the site with his heavies and taxing the residents. If they didn't pay up what he demanded, they would come home one day and find their trailers had been petrol-bombed. Scunthorpe was a small town and I knew the man in question. I also knew people who knew him and found out that he was planning to pay me a not-so-friendly visit when I moved in. I beat him to it and went straight to his house the day after I arrived on the site.

A man answered the door and straight away I cracked him in the face. I wasn't in the mood for conversation. He went down and I continued to beat him. I was taking all my frustrations out on his head and it felt good. It was a release from the tension I had been feeling. It was the first beating I dished out since Patrick's death.

In between blows the man was trying to say something. Eventually I stopped and let him have his say.

'It's not me you want, it's my brother,' he panted.

I heard someone in the house.

'Get out here, you fucking coward, and take your beating,' I yelled.

I knew that this man had been listening to his brother getting battered and hadn't come to help him out so it was safe to assume that he was scared. When he showed his face I told him I was there to sort out whatever problem he had with me and my site.

He looked at his brother who was bleeding badly. 'Let's forget this,' he said.

'I want your word you will leave that site alone and if you or any of your people come down there and make problems I will find you and kill you,' I told him. He agreed.

My life continued to descend into drink and drugs and grief. I'd given up. I was messed up big time. I stopped training and I stopped eating and I went from 17 stone to seven. I was skin and bone. I looked like a dead man. A few months after I went to Scunthorpe my father came to see me and he was shocked by what he saw. 'Hold your head up son,' he said. 'Never hold your head down. Don't bow your head for no one, don't cry and don't let anyone see your emotions.'

It killed me for my father to say that, because this was my son, how could I hide what I felt? The old man argued with me because I'd lost so much weight and he had an idea that I was taking drugs. He asked me outright and I denied it.

I spent my days in the local pubs and sometimes gravitated back to Manchester where I would disappear for a few days and get out of my head. Travellers would come to the pub to see me because I was a freak. I was a shadow at death's door. They'd come to see the great Paddy Doherty crying into his drink. Occasionally someone would rile me enough and I'd get in a fight but I had no pride left. I was ruled by anger and frustration. I wanted to be killed. I wanted to be hospitalised. I was on a massive spiral of self-destruction.

Roseanne and I continued to drift apart. We both grieved separately and we led separate lives. I hurt her. I wasn't there for her. I was looking for my own way out. I was so stupid and thick I didn't understand how she was feeling. I turned my back on her when I should have been by her side. She watched me destroy myself, she watched me shrink to a skeleton and piss away everything we had.

There was no money in the bank. I drank it all, but she didn't care. She just wanted me back, she wanted her Paddy. Everyone loved it. There was a lot of jealousy because we had been doing so well for ourselves and it came crashing down around our ears. People would say, 'Look at Roseanne now, she's not the woman she was' and 'Look at Paddy, he'll never come back from this'. I believed they were right. I always believed I could do wrong and I'd never be punished as long as I went to confessional in the morning. I robbed, I beat men half to death but after confessing the slate was wiped clean again and I was forgiven without reproach. In the months after Patrick died I felt like I was being punished for every sin I ever committed.

The Dohertys. (L-R: Tony, Francey, Barney, Simey Snr, Simey Jnr, Johnny, Hughie and me.)

All together. (Clockwise from top left: Davey, Simey Jnr, Simey Snr, me, Dudlow, Roseanne, Lizzie, Maggie and Martin.)

The last photo of my Par with his little brother Martin Tom.

Out with the boys, trying to hide the pain.

With my beautiful daughter Margaret on her wedding day.

My woman! My everything.

© TONY FISHER

Taken at the time of *My Big Fat Gypsy Wedding* – the start of a whole new life.

© JOHN PHILLIPS/REX FEATURES

Me and Thelma on the red carpet at the BAFTAs!

Never in my wildest dreams did I think a traveller could win *Big Brother*!

Having a laugh on
This Morning.

Taking Sally out for a
ride on my horse and
cart. I've never met a
woman like her!

Me now. Happy and proud.

18

Digging Deep

I broke myself on drugs and drink. I lost it all. Any money left over from the funeral went to feed my addictions. I didn't care at all. Roseanne would ask for money for things and I would just shrug. 'There isn't any,' I'd tell her.

She'd come to me and cry but I couldn't cry to her. I'd always been told not to show my emotions so I'd walk down the road and roar my brains out when I was alone.

Near where we lived there was an old gravel pit. It was a huge, ugly scar on the landscape that had become a dumping ground. It was bleak and dirty and muddy. A steep-sided crescent scoured out of a hillside where lorries now came and dumped piles of mud, junk and scrap. It became one of the places I went when I needed to be by myself. It mirrored the hole in my heart. I'd go down to the pit where no one could see me and scream at the top of my lungs. 'Why me? Patrick come back to me!'

I can't begin to imagine what I put the children through. They must have been scared seeing their daddy fall apart so spectacularly. But they never said anything because they loved me so much. They wouldn't question what I was doing and they didn't realise how selfish I was being. I didn't know how I was going to recover.

It took a combination of things to slowly start to wake me up.

The first was a newspaper ad. It was for applicants for the Manchester marathon in 1997. I read it when I was pissed in a pub one afternoon and a flicker of recognition crossed my mind.

'Shit, I have to apply for that,' I mumbled. I staggered home with the paper in my hand and the next morning when I was sober I realised the significance. I had a bet with Pat and I needed to honour it. I needed to run the marathon. I looked in the mirror. A skinny, pale, half-dead old man looked back at me.

'Fuck me,' I sighed. 'I'm going to need some training.'

It felt like a small light had switched back on inside me. I had a purpose. Later that day I put on a tracksuit and went for a run for the first time in months. As I ran out of the site people looked out their trailer windows at me. They couldn't believe I had got off my arse and was doing something. I managed a mile at best but I was determined to complete that marathon and prove to Patrick that I could do it. Each day I trained a little more and each day I felt a little fitter. The fog in my head was clearing gradually.

I still made regular trips to sit by Patrick's grave and I would talk to him there. I told him about the marathon. At the time I promised him that I would get him a headstone and it would be the biggest and best headstone any son ever had. The guilt I felt each time I went to his unmarked grave ate away at me. I had no money left to buy a memorial and I would never dishonour him with a cheap one. If I'd have asked my family for donations towards a headstone they would have happily helped out but I was too proud to beg and I didn't want people knowing just how much I'd squandered. In the end fate intervened.

Each day at 6 a.m. I went running and my course took me around the pit. Once it would have been no problem, but in my weakened state, it was a difficult route. The pit had steep sides and it was a challenge to get up and around it. Initially I'd get halfway and would have to stop. But as I got stronger, I managed to reach the lip of it and continue round. I noticed there were lots of bits of scrap buried in and around it.

One day as I was running across the pit I was stopped by a man who worked there.

He started talking to me. He was Irish and we fell into an easy patter.

He asked where I lived and I told him I was on the traveller site. He asked what I did for a living. I told him I dealt in scrap and I asked him about the metal buried in the earth that the lorries had dumped. I offered to buy it off him, even though I had no money to pay for it. 'It'll give me a few pound for me and my woman,' I said.

'I tell you what I'll do with you,' he said. 'You can have that bit of scrap for nothing if you get it out the ground and take it away.'

I thanked him and later in the day Simey and me went back in Patrick's lorry and loaded up. I gave the man the last £15 I had and said have a drink on me. He was thankful and I weighed the metal in for £100 at a nearby yard.

The next day I was running again and the man stopped me.

'You seem like a nice fella,' he said. 'What are you running for?' I told him about the marathon and the bet and I told him I had lost my son.

He thought for a while and then said: 'Come here three times a day and I'll have a load of scrap for you but you'll have to dig it out yourself.' I realised this was the way I could pay for Patrick's headstone.

For the next few months that is what I did. Each day I drove to the pit and I dug rusty metal from the ground, sometimes with my bare hands. I was working harder than I'd worked in years. It was backbreaking and I would be out in rain and snow. I would be covered in mud and grime. I'd cut my hands to shreds on rusty metal and I fell down the sides of the pit countless times. It was nothing like taking scrap from people's houses. The stuff was heavy, but sometimes I'd find a huge piece and lift it with the strength of ten men because I knew the money would pay for my son's memorial. The stock of scrap would be replenished daily because lorries would come with loads of earth to dump at the site and in amongst that would be the metal, which I would dig out. Sometimes I'd collapse with exhaustion but the next day I would be back again.

I was getting fitter. I didn't need drugs any more because they slowed me down. I turned my back on them and haven't touched them since. I got my appetite back and after a few weeks I was a stone heavier. Then another stone. Some days Simey came with me and I'd be digging out the metal while he loaded. Day in, day out we dug it up and weighed it in at the yard. We shifted tons of the stuff. We dug up fridges and ovens and bits of old cars. I went to the stonemason and ordered a headstone for £15,000 and kept going back at the end of every week to pay it off bit by bit.

Slowly the raw wounds were beginning to heal. I could feel Roseanne and me beginning to pull together as man and wife once again. I'd forgotten how close we were. I had missed my wife. I felt a slow reawakening, a realisation of how important my wife and family were. They were, are and always will be everything to me.

The first anniversary of Par's death came. I had been dreading it for weeks. It was like the funeral all over again. The emotional wounds were ripped open afresh. Roseanne and I couldn't stop crying all day and night. All my family came down from London where they were staying at the time. There were hundreds of people there. Our custom is to celebrate the life of the deceased and drink to their honour at the graveside but I just wanted to be alone. I couldn't drink, I couldn't stand it around me. I couldn't just put a happy face on, I was like a ghost. I shook hands and went through the motions but underneath I was dead. It was like I was a scratched record; I'd shake hands and say 'Thank you for coming' over and over again. The day couldn't end soon enough.

Every anniversary of his death since has been hard. As time goes by the pain changes. It doesn't stop hurting, it never will, but the sharp edges come off it.

Each year now Roseanne and I go to the grave and we have a good cry then we go back to the chalet and put on Patrick's CDs. I put my hand around Roseanne's back and we dance. I ask her, 'Sing me a song, woman' and we sing to each other. We'll never forget. We are a great help to each other now. Years ago I didn't realise what a help we could be. When Patrick died I turned my back on her but I realise now that she was always in my corner and always will be.

With the first anniversary gone I carried on working harder towards getting that headstone. I wanted something no one else had got and when I saw the finished piece I was overcome. It was black marble and beautiful. It had his picture and a picture of his car engraved in it. I got it myself with my own hands. It was the best money could buy and when it was put on the head of his grave it felt like Patrick was reborn and I felt redeemed. I knew that through God Patrick had made sure I was okay.

Things were becoming much clearer to me. I looked at Roseanne and suddenly realised how much she was hurting. We started talking again and we got closer to the way we were. I knew we still had some way to go but if we survived, nothing else would ever part us, only death. Now we are stronger together than we ever were. We are no good without each other, no matter what we say to each other or call each other. We argue like every couple. We row over silly things but we know they are only silly. I lost Patrick and lost my world. I believed nothing would be good again but in the end it really brought me and Roseanne together. I believe God spoke to Patrick and showed him me in the future, as I would have turned out had he not died. I would have got myself messed up on drugs, living in a council house or dead of an overdose. I was getting too big for my boots; I was getting cocky and carried away with my reputation. God said to Patrick 'If you don't come with me this is what will happen to your mummy and daddy.' All the fighting and the good living would have eventually corrupted me. It took Patrick's death and my subsequent decline to make me re-evaluate my life and see the error of my ways. Patrick decided to go with God because he knew that I had to get to the lowest point I could possibly go in order to get back up again.

19

Marathon Man

Just over a year after Patrick's death I took my place in the starting line-up for the Manchester marathon. I had trained for six months to be there and I was fitter and stronger than I had been for a long time. I trained every day and ate lots of food. I would eat carbs for energy and plenty of protein to build muscle. That's what made me put the weight back on. By the time I was ready for the marathon I was looking like my old self again. People would say, 'Scunthorpe is good for you.' I also felt better in my head. I trained all my life and it was good for my nerves. I could see a way forward. And family life was better because my kids had their daddy back.

The moment I woke on the morning of the marathon Patrick was in my head and my heart. I could feel him there willing me on. I put on the bracelet with the boxing gloves that he always wore. It had become my lucky charm.

At that time I didn't know of another traveller who had run a marathon. I was the first. I used the opportunity to raise money for a cystic fibrosis charity, in honour of my lost brother Francey.

I set off like a gazelle. For the first 15 miles I hardly broke a sweat. I ran like there was no tomorrow. Then as I crept towards the 18-mile mark I started to tire. My legs, back and shoulders ached. I pushed myself and I kept thinking of Patrick. I know he was there with me. I couldn't give in. I had never been a quitter and wasn't about to start. When I got to 20 miles I was running on willpower alone. But I didn't drop the pace. I didn't just want to finish the marathon. I wanted to do it in a respectable time.

My family came to cheer me on and on the way round they gave me a boost. My father came down, along with my brothers Hughie, Johnny, Simey, Martin, Davey and Dudlow. My mother was there too. I doubt there had ever been so many travellers in the crowd at a marathon.

The finish line was one of the sweetest things I had ever seen. As I struggled towards it I could see Roseanne in the crowd.

'Come on Paddy,' she was screaming. 'You can do it!'

Martin was there beside her, cheering me on. I was almost blinded by the sweat dripping into my eyes. I blinked it away and tried to give them a smile. It came out as a grimace.

Every muscle and tendon in my body was aching. I felt that if I stopped everything would seize up and I would never be able to walk again. I delved deeper than I had ever delved before for one last spurt of energy. It took every ounce of willpower I had to end the race in a sprint. I finished in under four hours and when I crossed the line I knew that Par was there with me, laughing and saying, 'You've earned your hundred quid there, Paddy.'

An hour later I was in the pub drinking with my family. It wasn't the recommended way to rehydrate but it's what Patrick would have wanted. Perhaps I should have warmed down and stretched properly afterwards, rather than get royally drunk because I couldn't walk for two days after that.

I may have been a hard man but I've always lived by the rules of fair play and I've always tried to help people less fortunate than myself. The Christian morals of doing unto others were embedded in me at an early age. It made me feel good to be able to do my bit for charity.

Things must have been improving because soon after the marathon Roseanne discovered she was expecting again. It was the final kick I needed to get my head straight. I knew I had to turn myself around for my woman and my children and I started picking up work where I could. Roseanne getting pregnant made me realise that life goes on and that there are many people in worse situations than I was. I tried to look at the positives. I was lucky. I had a great father and mother and children who were alive. I had a loving wife and brothers and sisters.

The fact that we had another child on the way wasn't the joyous occasion it would have been for other couples however. It filled us with apprehension. Once again there was a strong possibility that the child could die. The hospital confirmed our fears and told us that there was no way the baby would live. Again they advised that we terminate the birth but we wouldn't ever do that. And Roseanne was convinced that she could feel the child kicking. She got it in her head that the child was going to be alive and it messed with her emotions.

I pleaded with her to try and soften the blow when it was time for the baby to be born.

'Roseanne, the doctors know what's going on,' I told her. 'I'm so sorry, my darling, but the baby just won't survive.'

'I can't believe that's true,' she insisted, her eyes large and solemn in her lovely face, 'They're not right all the time. I just know that this baby will live, I know it.'

Some way into the pregnancy things started to go wrong. Roseanne was rushed to hospital in agony. The baby needed to come out. All my fears came to the surface. This wasn't like the other births. Roseanne was suffering. She was rushed to a treatment room and I ran behind and waited outside.

After a while a doctor came running out to speak to me. He looked flustered and concerned.

'It's touch and go, Mr Doherty,' he said.

'What's touch and go?' I frowned.

'We don't know whether your wife is going to make it,' he replied.

My stomach dropped. This couldn't be happening. Roseanne was my woman, the mother of my kids, and I couldn't lose her, not now, not after everything we had been through, not when we had started to rebuild the life we had before we lost Patrick. I had lost my first-born son. I was not going to lose my wife as well.

'Listen to me very carefully,' I said. 'My wife better make it or *you* are not going to make it. Go back in there and do whatever you have to do, because if you don't you are going to get it.'

I was deadly serious. I could not imagine living without her and I resorted to the only way of getting things done I knew; violence.

As we spoke nurses were ferrying bags and bags of blood into the room.

The doctor went back in. The waiting was agony and I could feel myself becoming more and more agitated. I kept running the worst-case scenarios over and over in my head, but I kept going back to one simple fact: I couldn't live without her. Roseanne couldn't die.

When the doctor came back out to give me an update and told me Roseanne was critical I told him if she died I would throw him out the window. We were 15 floors up.

I was just about to lose the plot. There would be no coming back for me if Roseanne died, I would lose everything, and I wouldn't care. And I just didn't feel like the doctor was doing enough. 'You don't understand,' I said. 'If my wife dies you are going to die and it means nothing to me if I get life in prison because life will not mean anything without her. Remember that one, doctor.' I'd even worked out that the children would be looked after by family if I went to prison. Roseanne and I were a link and the minute that broke she was no good and I was no good. I couldn't afford to lose her.

The bags of blood kept going in. What I didn't know at the time was that Roseanne lost ten pints of blood. They were using it up so fast it was coming straight from the chiller and they had to put it in a hot water tank to warm up so she wouldn't go into shock. She had no blood pressure and they had to tilt her legs up and her head down just to get the blood flowing through her.

After an hour the doctor came out. He looked relieved. 'I'm glad to say your wife is going to make it,' he said.

I put my hand on his shoulder. 'I'm glad to say you are going to make it as well,' I told him. It didn't register with him just how serious I was.

I went in to see her and she looked pale and tired. When she saw me she started crying. 'I'm sorry, my Paddy, I lost the baby,' she sobbed.

It had been a boy and like all the others who had died he had Fraser Syndrome. We agreed to call him Mylie.

'Don't worry, my Roseanne,' I said. 'As long as you are okay, that's all that matters.'

She was crying and we were holding each other. I had been through such a shock that by then I was screwed up in the head. She was on medication and drowsy and she looked at me and said, 'You need to bury the child, Paddy.'

'I'll do that, don't worry,' I said.

In my delirious state I assumed she meant, 'bury the child now', so I stayed with her a while until the medication took over completely and she fell asleep and then I left the hospital in a daze and set about the task of burying my child.

First I called my brother David and told him what had happened, that Roseanne nearly died and that we had to bury another child. 'I need you to come somewhere with me,' I explained.

'Of course, Paddy,' he said. 'Where do you want me to go?'

'To the graveyard,' I told him. It was night-time and I arranged to meet him at the locked gates at Gorton within the hour. 'Bring a shovel,' I added.

We met at the cemetery and David stared at me with a look of shock, pity and horror on his face. He didn't know what to say and instead followed me over the wall. I walked to the grave where Patrick was buried and I started to dig.

'What are you doing, Paddy?' David said nervously.

'Roseanne told me to bury the child so that's what I am doing. I want to do it before she comes out of hospital so she doesn't have the heartache again.'

David started trying to convince me it was the wrong thing to do but I told him not to worry and that no one would know.

'I'll get the child and I'll bury him here,' I said. I was going to rob the body out of the hospital.

David knew by this point that I was gone with the fairies. I was digging and digging down to my son for an hour until I heard a hollow *thud*. I reached the casket.

'Lovely, I've got it,' I said. I climbed out and went to get a slab to put over the hole.

David was crying at this point. I thought he was crying because the baby had died, not because I had lost my mind.

I went home and cleaned myself up and went to sleep.

The next morning I put my mud-stained clothes back on and went into town and into Debenhams because Roseanne had told me to get a teddy for Mylie. I found a beautiful cute penguin in the toy department and bought it. It was the nicest thing I could find for a newborn baby.

Then I realised I didn't have anything to bury the body in. I was walking around town in muddy clothes holding a toy penguin, trying to find a makeshift coffin for the body of a newborn baby. I walked past a cigar shop. It sold big Cuban ones. I went in and asked the man for his best box.

'How big do you want it?' he asked.

I did a quick calculation. 'Big enough to hold a couple of hundred cigars,' I said.

He handed over a lovely wooden box with a lid and I paid for it and then went off to collect my dead child from the hospital as if I was going off to get a pizza.

I went to the ward where Roseanne was and told one of the nurses that I had come to see my child. She was very sympathetic and arranged for me to visit the mortuary. I was escorted to a room and showed in by two women.

'I want to get my child out of here now. I am taking him,' I said.

'You can't do that, Mr Doherty,' one of the nurses explained.

'But I need to bury him,' I said.

They explained that I needed to get a death certificate from the records office.

'Okay, I'll be back in 20 minutes. Have him ready for me when I get back,' I said and walked out.

As I was trying to work out where the records office was I got a phone call. I recognised the voice on the other end of the line immediately. It was Sister Carmel. She was the travellers' nun. We all knew her and she'd been serving the traveller community for many years. When Sister Carmel spoke, you listened.

I asked her how she was and she said she was fine.

'How are you, Paddy?' she said. She sounded concerned.

'I'm fine,' I told her. I didn't want to tell her what I was up to. I said: 'Roseanne is fine and that's the main thing.'

'I need to see you, Paddy,' she said. I asked her what for.

'I can't tell you that on the phone,' she answered. 'Meet me in the graveyard.'

I had such a mixed-up head I didn't even think about the grave I had dug the night before and told her I'd be there as soon as I could. I drove to the graveyard and when I got there Sister Carmel was waiting by Patrick's grave with the gravedigger and David.

'Paddy, we have a problem,' she said. 'Someone has been trying to dig your son up.' The gravedigger moved the slab to show me the hole.

I'd been busted.

'I have a small confession to make,' I said. 'I did it.' I explained that I was going to get the child out of the hospital that afternoon and bury him.

'You can't do that,' Sister Carmel said.

'Why not? I'm putting my child with my other children,' I explained.

Sister Carmel was a slight Irish woman; short and lovely. She took me in her arms and gave me a hug. It's illegal,' she said. 'You have to do it properly, you have to go to the undertakers where you always go and they will sort it out for you and do it as fast as possible.'

By that time the undertaker knew me well, we were on first-name terms, and he told me how sorry he was when I explained about Mylie.

'I've already dug the hole,' I told him. And I gave him the box and asked him to put Mylie's body in it.

The undertaker looked at it and frowned.

'This is a cigar box,' he said. 'You can't put a baby in this.'

He showed me the range of baby caskets and I picked one out and gave him the penguin to put in it. When he explained that it would take two days to arrange and sort out the legalities I was disappointed. I felt like I had let Roseanne down. I went back to the hospital to see her.

'I couldn't bury the child,' I explained.

'What do you mean?' she asked, puzzled.

'You told me to bury the child. I tried but they wouldn't let me take him out the hospital,' I explained.

Roseanne stared at me. I think she realised I had cracked under the pressure.

The next day she got out and we buried Mylie. Trying to steal my child and bury him was the weirdest thing I ever did. It was the stress of nearly losing Roseanne. I didn't realise that I was having a mini-breakdown.

The list of children's names on my back was long by now and after we grieved for another dead child I took a trip to the tattoo parlour for a new addition. I was silent as I leaned forward and the tattooist began his work.

He knew by now not to talk to me. The only sound was the buzz of the needle as it etched the name of my child into my flesh. My back has become a living memorial to my children, living and dead. My own flesh is a canvas for me to remember them all by. I have Patrick's face on my chest and 'My Jesus' on my back.

Later that year, in October, we finally had a reason to celebrate as a family. My son Simey was the first of my children to get married. It was the first family function since Par's death and although it was a happy day, his loss was felt deeply. After the wedding we went straight to the graveyard and put the wedding bouquet on Par's grave. It was a custom all my children did over the following years as they each got married. My David, Johnny and Margaret did it and Martin Tom will do it when he gets married. It is a mark of respect to show that although he is dead, Patrick is not forgotten. He will always be part of our lives.

20

Home Sweet Home

The offer sounded like a good one.

'Come to Salford,' the council officials said. 'We've got a lovely site for you to look after, Paddy.'

It was another difficult camp that needed cleaning up, protecting and managing. It was in an industrial part of Greater Manchester; an area not known for its scenery or welcoming environment.

'I'm in,' I said.

It was 1998 and I needed a change. The Scunthorpe site was closing down and I was offered the chance to move back to the area I had grown up in. The site was big; there were around 30 pitches on it. The agreement was between Salford Council, the Gypsy Council and me. I was to look after it, collect rent, look after any maintenance issues and be a link between the residents and the authorities. Those were my official duties. Unofficially the residents were being taxed by local gangsters and I was going to make sure that stopped.

I didn't tell Roseanne that bit.

We had a lovely chalet right by the entrance gates and the first thing I did the day we moved in was write the letters 'PD' in white paint on the road by the gates. I was marking my territory. Anyone who wanted to go in there and cause trouble knew they were going to have to deal with me.

It didn't take long for trouble to find me.

After a few days a couple of hoodlums turned up, dripping in gold and designer clothes. I went outside to see what they wanted.

'We own this site,' they told me. 'There is a tax on living here.'

'Is there now?' I said. 'And how much would that be?'

They told me I would need to pay them £500 a month protection money.

I didn't care for them and I had never bowed down to any man in my life except God.

'I'm giving you nothing, you sausage, now fuck off, and you're getting nothing from anyone else on this site.'

That was the opening shot. I knew from experience that it wasn't going to be as easy as that. Sure enough, the next day I opened my front door and in broad daylight someone had come to the site and put five gallons of petrol in a tank on my doorstep. I knew what it meant. It was a warning. I was being told that any time they wanted to, they could come and burn my place to the ground.

Years of prizefighting meant I had good contacts in the Manchester underworld and it was easy to find out who the men were and more importantly who they were working for. I can't say his name but he was one of the country men gangsters who, at the time, ran Manchester with his brothers. My philosophy in life was never bother with the foot soldiers, go straight for the generals, so I got in my car and drove to the house of the man who was giving the orders to men who were threatening me. When I think about it now, it was insane. Anything could have happened to me. I could have easily ended up buried in a shallow grave somewhere, but I had no fear. I'd been at rock bottom and risen back to the top. I'd been hurt in unimaginable ways and still survived so a mere man was no trouble to me.

When I arrived at his door I was ready for war. It was answered by one of his brothers. He could see I meant business.

I told him I was the man on the site he was trying to tax and that his brother now had a problem with me that needed sorting. I was ranting, shouting and cussing. He knew I meant business and he was taken aback.

'Calm down, our kid will be down to see you,' he told me with the hint of a threat in his voice. He couldn't quite believe I had the front to knock on his door.

'You tell him to come and see me, anytime,' I told him. 'I'll be waiting for him.'

'Don't worry, pal. He'll be there in an hour,' the man said.

I turned and walked away, fired up with adrenaline. I was ready for whatever came my way and went back to the site to wait. I was sitting on the wall in front of my chalet three hours later when a man drove into the site in a convertible Mercedes. He drove past me and up and down the site between the caravans. I watched him go up the end, turn and come back down. He pulled up next to me and called out: 'Do you know where Paddy Doherty is?'

'He's here,' I told him.

The guy then jumped from the driver's seat out over the door. He did it in one fluid move, as though there was a spring in his seat that launched him into the air. I knew he had come to kill me but I was impressed.

I looked at him. 'Fucking hell, that was good!' I said. 'How did you do that?'

He ignored me.

'Paddy Doherty?' he asked, swaggering over to me. I stood from the wall to meet him head on, fixed him with a glare and nodded. I was ready for him.

'If you want to fight me, we'll have a one-to-one no problem. If you want a sword fight you get a machete and I'll get a machete and we'll have a machete fight. You want a gun fight and we'll have a gun fight,' I was giving him all the bluff talk. I had no knives or guns and I'd never used them in my life. It was all about psyching him out.

He was inches from my face with a look that said he meant business. Then he snorted, turned and walked back to his car.

Surely it wasn't going to be that easy?

He leaned over, reached under the seat for something and turned back around. There was a gun glinting in his hand.

He walked back towards me, raised it and held it right in the middle of my head. It wasn't the first time someone had pulled a gun on me and it probably wouldn't be the last. I wasn't intimidated and I pressed my head into the muzzle and growled.

'You better use that and blow my brains out because if you don't you and your pals are dead.'

'I'll fucking kill you!' he threatened.

The gun was making a dent in my forehead he was pushing it so hard. I kept telling him to pull the trigger and he kept telling me he would. He was getting tenser and tenser.

In the middle of the exchange, at the point where something had to give – either he had to pull the trigger and make good on his threats or walk away – his phone rang. It was the old Nokia ringtone. It was almost comical.

The man looked at me and while he was still holding the gun in my right hand, answered his phone with his left.

'I'm here,' he said into the receiver. I heard the voice on the other end. The gunman talked. 'No not yet... I don't know, I'll ask him,' he said.

'Are you Paddy Doherty from Mancunian side?' he asked.

'Yeah, why?' I replied. Greater Manchester is divided into two sides, Manchester and Salford; for much of my life I had lived on the Manchester side.

The man told the voice on the phone that I was, nodded, looked at me and lowered the gun.

'For fuck's sake, we didn't realise you were *that* Paddy Doherty, we thought you were a different one. Our kid knows you well,' he smiled.

He put his arm round me and laughed. Thanks to my links, one of the family, a cousin, knew me well and was aware of my reputation. He'd heard about the mad gypsy who had fronted up the main man and called in to check whether it was me.

'I tell you what, Paddy, you've got some balls,' the gunman said.

'You've got some balls too, holding a gun to me,' I told him.

'You really didn't give a damn did you?' he said. 'You'll never know how close you came to having your brains taken out.'

God must have been looking after me that day. I learnt later that the man sent to kill me was known for having an itchy trigger finger. He drove off chuckling to himself. I relaxed and went back indoors like nothing had happened. Roseanne had been watching it all in horror from the front window and began crying and wailing when I walked in.

'You mad bastard, you are going to make me a widow,' she wept.

'He wouldn't have done anything. He was a sausage,' I lied.

When she calmed down I sent her to the shops to get some food and when she left the house everything kicked in. It must have been an adrenaline crash because I was shaking and my arse went like a wacker-plate. I lost about a stone there and then!

My reputation had saved me. I'd arrived at the site without fanfare and no one knew me there. But I had a name like a race-horse over on the Mancunian side, and reputation soon spreads. I got to know all the right faces and soon learnt that the people in Salford were a special breed. There was a community there the type of which I hadn't come across before. I joined the local gym, Flex N Tone. It was a proper gym, with a boxing ring, and run by hard and fair men: Mike, Steve, Lee and Tony. They became good friends with me and my family. All my boys used the gym too.

I had a few scuffles with some of the local hard nuts but I soon became part of the community. I'd eat daily at the Top

Scram café and Salford became more of a home to me in the following years than anywhere else I had ever lived. For the first time in my life I felt settled.

I laid down the rules for the site I was running. No family could live there unless they sent their children to school. They'd get three or four chances and if they continued to keep their children off I'd tell them to leave.

'If you want to be thick and ignorant I'll be thick and ignorant with you,' I'd tell them. In my opinion it was selfish to not send kids to school and not want them to mix with country folk or to read or write. It should be an honour for a child to read.

I also sorted out arguments. I settled fights and got feuds squashed before they had a chance to develop. I was the mediator. People would come to me to sort out their problems. Most Saturday nights there would be a knock on the door and I would be needed to deal with some minor domestic drama. When I wasn't there and people came to the chalet to ask me to deal with a problem, Roseanne would have to go and try to stop it. There would be fights and people would be knocking litres of blood out of each other and she would be standing there shouting, 'Come on, now, you've got to stop this.' In a way, they put me up on a pedestal, but in a good way. I didn't order the residents around and make up unreasonable rules. I didn't throw my weight around. They respected me because I developed a reputation for being fair. It was an honour to be respected like that. I was beginning to learn that you didn't always have to use your fists to get through to people. The reputation I had bled to achieve had become so well-known that I needed to prove myself less and less.

There were men in that city I admired greatly because of their reputation for fair play. Some of them I'd fought in the past and at that time I could see myself becoming like them. I knew I couldn't keep fighting for ever. Since Patrick died I'd been fighting less and less. I started to think that perhaps I could be a fair play man. One of the greatest fair play men in Manchester was Patrick 'Snick' Kiely. He is dead now, God rest his soul, but at one time he ran Manchester. If you wanted a fight you had to go through him. He was a gentleman and over the years me and him had disagreements and fights but he was honourable beyond words and I looked up to him and hoped I could have the reputation that he had. The century was turning, I was 40, times were changing and I wasn't getting any younger.

Just before moving to Salford I even became a grandfather for the first time. Simey had his first child, a son. When I heard the news about the birth of course I was delighted, but in the back of my mind I still had the thought that it should have been Patrick having the first child.

Simey and his wife Donna called the baby Patrick, not after me but after Par.

21

My Margaret

Within the traveller community there's a lot of bemusement about the country folks' fascination with our weddings. Thanks to television, we seem to have gained a reputation for the biggest and most colourful ceremonies you could ever see. Much of what you see and hear on the TV is right. Some traveller weddings are huge affairs, with glass carriages, helicopters and armies of colourfully dressed bridesmaids. But just as many are low-key affairs. At the end of the day it all depends on money and how much the family – mainly the father of the bride – has to spend. Sometimes marrying couples have the option of taking a lump sum in place of a big ceremony. Because of this, sons are worth a fortune.

Many gypsies marry cousins and second cousins to ensure that family money passes to family and stays within their particular clan. Footing the bill for a wedding can also be an investment for a father because his new son-in-law may be worth a lot of money.

In 2001 my Margaret got married and it was my turn to stage my own Big Fat Gypsy Wedding. I wanted the best for her. She was my only surviving daughter, and while Roseanne is my woman, Margaret will always be my girl.

Her husband-to-be, John, must have been crapping himself when he came to me to ask for her hand. He knew how close we were and he knew what would happen if he ever did anything to hurt her. They had been going steady for a while and they were in love with each other. John came to meet me in the pub to ask my permission. He'd dressed up and looked smart and nervous.

I knew what was coming because he'd told Simey and Simey came and told me. John is Margaret's second cousin. His parents are lovely people and they had raised him well.

John approached me at the bar. 'Paddy, can I have a word with you?' he asked.

'What is it, John?'

He blurted it out. 'I love Margaret and I want to marry her.'

I fixed him with a stare. For several seconds I said nothing.

Then I asked him: 'Are you sure about that, John?'

He nodded his head. 'Yes, Paddy, I am. Why?'

'Because if you ever hurt my daughter your life won't be worth living,' I told him. 'I'll kill you. I'll beat you to death. As long as you realise that, things will be fine.'

John gulped and nodded his head. I admired his balls.

'You must love her very much,' I said.

'Yes, I do,' he replied.

I was then faced with the choice. Whatever I chose would be expensive. I could either go all out and pay for a big affair or I could give them money to start their life together. Either way my standing in the community meant that people would be expecting a big statement.

I sat with John and explained his options.

'I can give you the best wedding that money will ever buy or I can give you a big lump sum that you can put in the bank, and I'll give you a normal wedding. It's your choice,' I said.

John didn't have to think too long about it. 'Paddy, I want the full Monty,' he said.

'Shit,' I thought, 'that's going to cost me.'

Margaret and Roseanne set about organising the day. The reception venue was a manor house just outside Salford. We wanted to have something different, something no traveller wedding had ever had, and settled on the idea of fireworks. But not just any display. We were going to light up the sky over the city. We got in touch with a fireworks expert and gave him a budget. I won't say how much but the fireworks had to be specially imported from America and the display was scheduled to go on for over an hour. I told the venue that I planned to let a few rockets off in the evening, no big deal, and it wouldn't upset their neighbours. I knew I'd probably need planning permission for what I really had in mind. On the day it took the pyrotechnics man four hours to set up the explosions and they had to be electronically controlled.

When I walked Margaret down the aisle I was equally proud and sad. It broke my heart to give her away. She had grown into a beautiful woman, but John was a good man and he had promised to take care of her.

After she said her vows we went to Gorton and Margaret, Roseanne and I stood in front of Par's grave. It was a beautiful warm summer's day. There was a gentle breeze blowing in the trees and it was a quiet sanctuary after the hubbub of the wedding. John was there, but he was standing some way off, giving us the distance that we needed.

Margaret bent down and laid her bridal bouquet on Patrick's grave while I leaned forward and kissed the cool stone. When she stood up, tears were running down her face, and I could hear Roseanne sobbing quietly on the other side of me. I also felt tears welling up in my eyes, but I blinked them back. I had to be strong. Today was about celebrating, not about mourning.

'Hey,' I said quietly, brushing away the tears from Margaret's cheek. 'Don't be sad. This is your day.'

'Daddy,' she said, 'I just miss him I wish he was here.'

'He is here. He's with you always,' I urged. 'And he'd never want you to be sad, not on this day. We all miss him. I know he's up there, looking down on us all.'

Roseanne put her arm around Margaret's shoulders and led her to the waiting car. I watched my two beautiful women walk away from the grave with a mixture of pride and sadness

You can never tell how many people turn up to gypsy weddings, but there were easily 2,000 at the reception. There was a free bar and inevitably there was a bit of trouble. I got in an argument with a guest who had come looking for a fight. He'd had a few drinks and was bragging about fighting Doherty men.

'I've beat every Doherty,' he was telling people.

To show such disrespect to the host of a wedding was unforgivable.

'You need to come outside,' I told him. And like the idiot he was he followed me outside.

We squared up in the car park and I hit him with an almighty hook that connected straight to his jaw. I wasn't in the mood for messing around and I didn't want the man to take up any of my time. It was my daughter's day and he wasn't going to ruin it. His legs went straight from under him and he crumpled. But he didn't go down. He seemed to hang in the air.

That's strange, I thought, and I gave him another dig, then another. His head was lolling around as I hit it and it was clear that he was spark out but he wouldn't go down. Then I realised what had happened. As he'd fallen the crook of his arm had caught on the car bonnet he'd fallen against and he was hanging there. I left him and turned to go back inside.

As I did his brother came out.

'Who's knocked out my brother?' he shouted. He was swaggering like he meant business. Or perhaps he was swaggering because he was drunk.

'I did, and I'll knock you out too,' I said. As I finished the sentence I swung the same punch at his face and it made a *crack* as it connected. He went straight down, just as if this was a cartoon and I had hit him with an anvil. I had to laugh – what's a gypsy wedding without a punch up? At least this was entertainment that I didn't need to pay for!

Later that evening, when it got dark, the bar closed momentarily and everyone was led outside. In the distance our fireworks expert flicked a switch and lit up the sky. The colours exploded across the city. Rockets screamed into the sky and exploded. Circles of blues, reds and greens spread across the horizon. Roseanne stood next to me and I reached out and squeezed her hand. She looked up at me and I saw the lights from the sky reflecting in her eyes.

'You look beautiful,' I mouthed. It was a fairytale day and I was so happy, happier than I had been for a long time.

It was an amazing display. The ground shook with a thunderous finale and everyone cheered. The people who ran the venue didn't know what to do. Once the display had started there was nothing they could do to stop it. All they could do was watch and hope the neighbours weren't too annoyed. I doubt they would have been. Salford had rarely seen anything so spectacular.

That set the standard. Following Margaret's wedding everyone wanted fireworks and now any big traveller wedding will have a firework display. Venues have got wise to it and keep a special eye on what's being prepared in their grounds.

Travellers do like to improve on what's gone before. At one time it was the big cakes. Cakes just seemed to get taller and taller and brides would compete to see who could get the most tiers. If you were a cake-maker and you got an order from a gypsy you knew you were in for a good payday. My sister Mary had a 34-tier cake and they got even bigger than that. After cakes it was the dresses. I look at the dresses the brides wear now and remember back to the one my Roseanne wore on our wedding day. They are like chalk and cheese. Weddings are big events for travellers and they give the younger girls a chance to go out and dress up and mix with other travellers.

A lot gets made by country folk about the way young girls dress but to the girls it's about competition. It's about looking the best. They are all very innocent. There's nothing wrong with them getting dressed up and wearing make-up once or twice a year at a wedding when they are with their own people. It's not as if they go out all the time, and the clothes are just copied from what they see their heroes wear in music videos.

The girls lead innocent lives and they love their families and although many people don't understand, they like their lives. Our women like being at home cleaning and cooking and looking after children. My Margaret is happy with her life. From the minute she gets up in the morning to the minute she goes to sleep all she does is clean. Roseanne is the same. They take huge pride in their homes. They love it, they become junkies for cleaning; they are cleaning fanatics. And why is that so wrong if they are happy doing it?

People have a misconception that travellers are dirty and that couldn't be further from the truth. For a gypsy woman to be thought of as dirty is a huge dishonour to her. So they take a lot of pride in their turnout, in their possessions, they way they look and their homes. I was always taught that first impressions are everything. Right back from when I had to knock on doors asking for scrap I realised that the better you look, the more people will think of you. I always make sure I am smart and presentable. I like the best things in life. I like clean new shirts, I get all mine from a shop called Jean Image in Cheatham Hill, Manchester and I've been going there for years. Clothes don't make the man but they give an indication of the type of man you are.

When Margaret moved out she never left us. She still hasn't. She lives on the same site we do, next to our plot. She's my only surviving daughter and very precious to me. I've never let go of her and I never will.

Only Martin Tom is unmarried now. David got married in 2002 and Johnny got married in 2005. All my children are married to traveller girls and they live the traveller life. They are proud of their heritage. It's the way they have been brought up. Our ways are dying out. You get a lot of travellers going to live with country folk and a lot of country folk who think they are travellers, mock travellers. They don't know who they are. It's sad that such an old way of life is slowly disappearing but I'm thankful my sons and my daughter carry on the tradition within my family.

I would never stop them doing something they wanted to do, though. If one of my kids wanted to live the country life there would be nothing I could do. I'd be sad but you rear your children a certain way and then they fly away from the nest and if they choose not to live the way you have shown, that is their decision. In truth, if they do that and they are happy then good luck to them. If my Martin Tom married a country woman and they lived in a house I'd love her just as much as I love my Margaret. Years ago I may have said no way would any child of mine ever marry a country person, not in a million years, but then I heard Martin Tom talking one day. He said he could never meet a country woman, because I wouldn't allow it. When I heard him say that it made me sad. What if he met a woman and fell in love with her but couldn't tell his mummy and daddy? His heart would be broken. It wouldn't be fair. So later I told him: 'Martin, you go with whoever you are happy with and don't get married until you know she is the perfect woman. When you marry you marry for life.'

I've been married over 30 years now but that's not a long time for a traveller. When I first met Roseanne I valued being in her company so much that the days weren't long enough. They still aren't.

22

The Fair Play Man

There comes a time in every man's life when you have to take stock of who you are, where you are, and what you want your future to be. At the age of 42 I'd lived life to the full. I'd seen more death and destruction than most people experience in a lifetime. I'd had my heart torn out and I should have died more times than I could recall.

On the one hand I'd suffered massive misfortune but on the other, I'd been one lucky bastard. I knew what it felt like to be at rock bottom; there had been times when I was so low, just dragging myself out of bed in the morning seemed like a superhuman task; they were the times when I wanted to roll over and die. But I never could. It was never bred into to me to be a quitter and no matter how hopeless things appeared, I always carried a seed of hope in my heart that times would get better and that I would beat the thing that was keeping me down.

In my fighting career I had been beaten to within an inch of my life. I'd swallowed pints of my own blood. I'd broken bones and in turn my bones had been broken. Scars criss-crossed my face and body.

I'd fought the best, I'd beaten the best and I'd been the best. But you can only walk the path I had walked down for so long and since Patrick died I had been less and less interested in going out and looking for trouble. It often found me, and I was still a man to be feared, but the aggressive hunger for recognition and the fascination for violence that fuelled me in my twenties and thirties had begun to wane. I'd never roll over and I would never let another man disrespect me, but I started to think about getting out the organised-fight game for good. I was getting older; if I was honest with myself I was past my prime. I had fought all my life to gain the reputation I had and didn't have to prove myself to anyone any more.

Roseanne had been on at me for years. She hated what I did but understood there was nothing she could do about it. She knew who I was and what I was and although she never fully accepted it, she knew she couldn't change me.

I wanted to enjoy what I had left of my life. I had grandchildren and family and the older I got, the more that meant to me and the more I wanted to be around to see them all grow up. Gradually the fighting became less and less until eventually I got out the fighting game almost completely.

I knew there would be people who would criticise me for it and would say that I was no longer up for it. I didn't care what they said. I had nothing to prove to anyone and I'd still give a man a hiding if need be. But the old fighting ways were changing, and I didn't much like what I saw.

Today my generation are all trying to keep the kids in line. The youngsters have all gone a bit wrong. All the old men have the same morals and codes but our sons and their sons no longer fight fair. Now arguments and feuds get sorted out with guns and knives and fighters use drugs. Fighting men today are not the kind of men we were. We were 100 times better than them. Now they shoot up with steroids to get angry. It's all false.

In my day and my father's day you had fighters who would beat each other half to death but would still shake hands and buy each other a drink afterwards because they respected each other. Without respect the fight scene is a very dark place indeed. These old fighting ways are finished now, they are dying off. My generation is like video, we are being replaced by DVD and Blu-Ray.

However, even though I had made a decision to get out of fighting, fighting would never entirely leave me. You can take the Doherty out of the fight but you can never take the fight out of the Doherty. I was born for it and, having been one of the best-known gypsy fighters of my generation, it was hard to turn my back on it entirely. It followed me. You can't have the type of reputation I had and disappear completely.

Instead, as I fought less I was asked more and more to be a fair play man. I began to gain a reputation as someone who could be relied on to show fairness to both fighters. In my way I was able to make sure the code of morals I was brought up to adhere to was carried on. It started with small fights and disagreements on the site in Salford. If there were two men who had a beef with each other they would knock on my door and ask me to show fair play. Some people will no doubt argue that you should never resort to violence to settle a disagreement. I say bollocks. Sometimes, and for a certain type of person, violence is the only way and it's the best way. In a fair fight the problem is settled there and then, it's not allowed to develop into something worse.

After officiating at several smaller fights I was asked to London to be the fair play man at a bout between two well-known men in the traveller community. It was between a McDonagh and a Ward. They were both my people. Gypsy families are tied together through blood and marriage. People often marry distant cousins and extend their family name, like a clan, and these men were relatives of mine. Because they both knew me and knew my reputation they asked for me. One man lived in Ireland and the other lived in England. Both parties needed to be happy with the choice of fair play man. When I got the call it was a real honour. You don't apply to be a fair play man, the job comes to find you, and it finds you because people respect you. Both the fighters knew that I would show no favouritism. As a fair play man I could be refereeing a fight between my own son and a stranger and I would still remain totally neutral.

The fight took place in the Scrubs in Hammersmith. I had fought there several times over the years. I drove to the capital and stayed overnight, ready for the early start the following morning.

When I arrived the area was packed. Travellers had come from all over the country and many had travelled across from Ireland. There were plenty of faces I knew in the crowd. The fighters were two big men. They were bare-chested but had crepe bandages wrapped around their knuckles. In theory the bandages are there to protect knuckles but fighters used crepe ones because they are rough; like sandpaper. They are very dangerous because they cut. Some people say it is cheating but it's within the rules.

I checked under the bandages for rings because a lot of fighters will pad out heavy rings with cotton wool, which compresses as the fight progresses to reveal sharp edges.

Once I was satisfied that the fighters were not concealing anything I waved the fight to start. The two men started fighting and within a few minutes one of them was cut. It was a wide gash across the bridge of his nose. He looked like he had been slashed with a Stanley knife. He was bleeding everywhere. Each time he was getting punched, more blood smeared across his face.

'You look a mess,' I told him, 'Do you want to stop?'

'No thanks, Paddy, this fight is only just opening up,' he said.

They fought on and the cut man's face was getting bloodier and bloodier. He kept going, though, and despite the look of him I could see he had plenty left in the tank. I let the fight continue and he began to get into his stride. After about 20 minutes, just as the other man was tiring, he started to fire off fierce combination shots with pinpoint accuracy. After a savage flurry he knocked his opponent down. I was a seasoned fighter and as the man got up shaking the fog from his head I could see that his will had gone. He thought the fight was in the bag, he had used up all the energy he had and he knew he was wide open for a beating. But he was a proud man and I knew he wouldn't give best. The next shot caught him square on in the mouth. It snapped his head back so violently I thought his neck was going to break, and as his head arched back I saw the front teeth fly out of his mouth still attached to the bloody clump of gum they were embedded in. The whole fleshy package had been ripped from his mouth.

The teeth and gums landed right in front of my feet. The man went down holding his mouth. Blood flowed freely through his fingers. I looked down and could see the black nerves hanging from the root of the teeth, which were poking out the bottom of the pink gum. I stared and the nerves twitched in the grass. I'd seen some horrible things in my time, but that was the freakiest sight I had ever laid eyes on.

The toothless man was beaten and was taken to hospital with his detached teeth for some emergency dental work. I had received my first introduction to the joys of being a fair play man.

Since that day I've overseen hundreds of fights. I was soon in demand and, as in my fighting days, my reputation went before me. I travelled throughout the country and to Scotland, Wales and Ireland to show fair play to every sort of traveller, to country people against country people and gangster against gangster, because they have their morals as well.

I always endeavoured to say yes when I was asked. In a way I hoped that by making sure the old rules were followed, I could still preserve some of the traditions that I grew up to respect and follow.

The only rule I had was that both fighters had to ask me. Sometimes I got letters and sometimes DVDs and videos. It was quite common for people to send each other tapes when they wanted to arrange a fight. They would sit in front of a camera or a webcam and explain who they wanted to fight and why. Often the whole family got involved and took turns. The tape then got sent and the opponent replied with his own recorded message. Those recordings were sent to me so I knew who was fighting and what the argument was about. Often they were people I have never met.

'We want Paddy Doherty to be the fair play man,' they said, 'because he is the fairest man of all.'

It was always an honour to hear those words.

23

The Day I Died

I've stared down the barrel of a gun four times in my life. I was lucky three times. On one occasion a phone call saved me. On another I was with my brother Martin in a pub when a gunman walked in and I stood in the way. He raised the weapon towards me and before he had a chance to cock it and fire it I knocked him out. He was a sausage. I knew by the look of him he would never have used it. The third time I got away by the skin of my teeth. By the fourth time I truly believed I was immune. I thought bullets couldn't hurt me. I was wrong.

The third time led to the fourth time. There was a family feud. I had an argument with two brothers. The argument started over our sons. I knew the family well, I won't name names out of respect for the dead, but the ill feeling escalated and a fight with one of the brothers broke out. After the fight the matter was closed as far as I was concerned but the man kept pushing so I went for a rematch. I drove to his house. I wasn't going to pussyfoot around, I turned up on his doorstep and I wanted to knock him out.

When he answered the door he had a gun. I wasn't in the mood for messing around.

'You pull that on me and you better be prepared to use it,' I told him.

He wouldn't step out from inside his house and stood there in the doorway threatening me.

'Come out and fight like a man,' I demanded.

'I'll finish you, Paddy Doherty, you dirty black bastard,' he was shouting. He knew the old buttons to press. He was waving the gun around as if it was a toy.

I knew he wouldn't come out and fight me so I turned my back to him and got in the car to drive away. I had a Mercedes at the time and as I pulled off I saw him run out his door in the rear-view mirror. I slammed my brakes on, then saw him raise his arms. A split second later the back windscreen shattered into a million pieces. The glass blew out and I felt a shockwave of compressed air pulse through the car.

Maybe he was serious after all. I put my foot down and as I sped off I let out a howl of laughter. It was a rush. I'd just dodged a bullet like a cowboy in the Wild West.

I was stupid and reckless. It didn't register with me that my wife could have been widowed and my children left fatherless. I just thought it was funny. I had no fear and guns were useless against me.

There was a witness to the shooting. Someone in the road saw what happened and called the police. They got my registration number and a few hours later the cops were on my doorstep. They could see my car had been shot and they questioned me and asked me who it was. They tried to get me to make a statement against the man but I told them I didn't know who he was. I'd never cooperate with the police; I preferred to sort out my problems my way. For my troubles I was arrested and taken in for questioning. Still I said nothing and eventually they let me go. They couldn't charge me with anything. Being shot at isn't a crime. The man, however, didn't get off. Because there was a witness he was charged and found guilty of letting a firearm off in a public place.

So at that point we'd gone from a verbal row to a fight to an attempted shooting to a criminal conviction. Logic should have told the man to stop at that but he couldn't. Instead he sent his brother to try and deal with me.

It was 6 October 2003; a dull autumn Monday morning and I was taking Martin Tom to school. He was nine and all dressed up in his uniform. As we walked out the front door I saw a van pull up outside the chalet and the brother got out of the driver's door. I knew him. He walked across the front yard with his hand in his pocket.

'I'm gonna shoot you. My brother told me to shoot you in the head and that's what I'm going to do,' he ranted.

I could see he meant business. I moved Martin Tom out the way and shoved him towards the door.

'Go in, son,' I told him.

When I looked back up from my son's face the man was directly in front of me with a gun in his hand. I looked in his eyes and I could see fear and determination there. He kept repeating, 'I'm gonna fucking shoot you!'

'And I'm going to take that gun off you and stick it up your arse!' I yelled.

I had nothing to fear from him. I had faced up to bigger bullies than him before and come out on top. And to look at him, well, he was nothing much. He was shaking.

I decided to call his bluff. 'If you're going to shoot me, then shoot me,' I snarled. 'I don't think you've got it in you. You don't have the balls to pull the trigger.'

The man had sweat dripping down his forehead, he was looking left and right as if he was trying to find a way out. He was scared of me, and he was the one with the gun.

I took a step towards him. Stupidity or bravado, I don't know which, but I wasn't going to back down. I could see his finger on the trigger; I could see the black hole of the raised barrel. And then? And then I was shot. He shot me out of fear not guts.

I don't remember what the shot felt like. There was no pain, just a dull impact. The bullet went through the middle of my forehead into my skull. I went down like a sack of spuds. It was like someone flicked the off switch. Martin ran inside screaming for Roseanne.

'Daddy's dead,' he was shouting.

The gunman ran back to his van and sped out of the site. Roseanne heard the shot and Martin Tom's screams and ran out to see me lying on the floor in a kneeling position, face down. My forehead was resting on the concrete step at the front of my door. My eyes were open but no one was home. There was a hole in the centre of my head. Wisps of smoke drifted out of it and a small cascade of burning gunpowder dripped from it onto the stone and burnt a circle on it.

Roseanne was roaring and she turned me over. She started beating my chest exactly the same way she did with Patrick. 'Don't die, my Paddy!' she screamed. 'You can't die.'

I know all this happened even though I was unconscious because I was no longer in my body. I was dead and I was floating above the scene. I was watching the scene unfold and telling Roseanne: 'Don't be a sausage, I'm not dead. I'm here. I'm okay.'

A man from the site heard the commotion and came over. He looked at me on the ground and put his arm on Roseanne's shoulder.

'Paddy's gone, he's dead,' he told her.

'I'm not dead, I'm alive,' I was calling. I couldn't understand what was happening to me. I was looking down at myself on the floor.

By that point someone had called the emergency services but no ambulance could get onto the scene because firearms were involved and the police needed to be sure that there was no danger. So for several minutes Roseanne and Martin Tom were left there, stricken, with my body while I watched. When the scene was secure the ambulance came in. Then it started to get dark. It felt like the shutters were coming down and that's when it hit me, I was dying. It was the blackest black you could ever imagine. And it put the fear of God in me. I said a prayer: 'Please, my Jesus, forgive me for everything I've done and have mercy on my soul.' Then the blackness enveloped me and took me under.

The next thing I remember is convulsing on the ambulance gurney as the defibrillator sent 500 volts through my heart. My body went into shock and I started to shake violently. The paramedics strapped me down. I was calling for Roseanne and she was in there with me but I was only half aware of what was going on.

At the hospital I was rushed into surgery with a bullet lodged in my brain. The skin on my forehead was cut away from the bone and pulled back to expose my skull which was cracked open like a hard-boiled eggshell. The surgeons skilfully removed the bullet and cleaned round the wound. I was told later that what saved me was the way I fell. Because I fell forward, the gunpowder fell out of the wound. If it had stayed in the hole it would most likely have burned my brain.

I had cheated death again, but when I came round I didn't feel lucky. I was swathed in bandages and confused. And there was my family: Roseanne, David and Margaret, Simey and Martin Tom. They were all there. I will never forget the look on their faces – deep worry combined with relief.

'Oh Paddy, my Paddy, I thought we had lost you,' Roseanne sobbed, 'I thought you were dead. I thought I would never see you again.'

I could barely speak, but deep down I knew that Roseanne couldn't face this again. She had been through too much. Fighting with fists, that was one thing, but solving differences with guns, well, that was not the traveller way.

This couldn't go on. How could I fight with honour when the people who wanted to fight me weren't honourable men?

Almost immediately after I was admitted to hospital the visitors started to come. Travellers from every corner of the country came to see me and pay their respects. There was a constant procession. Ned Rooney, my old sparring partner, was on the way to America when I was shot. He heard what had happened when he landed and got on the next plane back to the UK to see me.

My old man came to see me. I was in intensive care at that point. I was fading in and out of consciousness with machines monitoring me. Half the time I didn't know what I was talking about. But I knew enough to know I had been shot and I knew who did it. I wanted to even the score and I told my father so.

'This has gone too far now,' I explained. 'I can't cope with this shooting. I want you to set it up so we have a fair fight and that will be the end of it.'

The old man looked at me and shook his head.

'Are you mad?' he asked. 'You are lying here in a hospital bed. You've just been shot in the head and now you want to fight?'

'I'll be all right in six weeks,' I offered.

'Will you shut up and forget about the fight,' he said.

When I was out of intensive care I was put in a room on my own and Roseanne stayed with me. I was happy then because I had my woman and I was alive. A few days after I came round, for the first time in my life, fear kicked in. I knew that I could get hurt and I could die. I faced up to my own mortality. I realised I wasn't immune and it was the best thing that ever happened to me. Before that day I was a very dangerous man, not just to myself but to those around me. I never thought about the consequences of my actions and my arrogance in the face of danger. I never considered what impact my death would have had on my family and loved ones. It took a bullet in my brain to make me re-evaluate my life. I knew I couldn't carry on taking the type of risks I had taken all my life. It was a certainty that one day my luck would run out. The thought of that blackness descending on me again filled me with dread.

It wasn't just the psychological effects of the shooting that stayed with me. The physical effects lasted for many months. My brain did strange things. One day I was chatting to Roseanne in the hospital and I began to flip out. I felt hands inside my skull! I started calling out. 'Woman, my head's moving, get the doctor,' I screamed. It felt like it was moving back and forth. It was the weirdest thing I've ever felt.

I was gripping the side of the bed and tensing my neck to try and steady myself but whatever I did it still felt like my head was swaying. The doctor came and explained that it wasn't moving. He got a mirror and held it up.

'See, Mr Doherty, your head is perfectly still,' he said. But no matter what I saw it felt as if it was moving. I was crying. I thought I was going mad.

'Is the motion back and forward and down over your eyes?' the doctor asked.

'Yes,' I replied.

He explained that it was an imprint of the motion the surgeons had used when they operated and cleaned my brain after the surgery. They had used their hands to clean around my brain and remove the gunpowder and debris. My brain remembered it and was replaying it. He explained that every so often I would have those episodes and that it could repeat itself for up to two years and longer.

'You'll always feel those hands,' he said.

He was right, for years afterwards I would be sitting somewhere doing something and suddenly I'd feel a hand moving around my brain. My nervous system was all messed up.

The shooting made the papers and for many months afterwards there was talk in the traveller community about how Paddy Doherty was going to get his revenge. But the incident changed me on a fundamental level. Fear wasn't the only thing that I discovered. I also found God again. Religion had always played a big part in my life. The church was always there in the background. When I was a kid I took communion every Sunday and spent Sundays as an altar boy and then at Sunday school. The church was there to support me when each of my children died and to gently steer me back to normality when I tried to steal the body of my baby. I knew God loved me and started going to church regularly again with Roseanne, and I have never looked back. Every time I ask God to help me, he helps me. No matter how you look at it and even if you do not believe in it, it does no harm. We all need help in our lives and if you say, 'Please, my God, help me,' and say it from your heart, even if you are not into religion, he might just come to you. God never sleeps, he hears everybody.

Now I thank God for every day I have. I had a near-death experience and came out of my body and that blackness I went through was the most frightening thing I had been through. I died and God gave me life back.

24

Britain's Deadliest Man

Up until a few years ago travellers had always kept themselves to themselves. We lived our lives behind the walls of our sites and were shunned by country folk. The prejudices of the past drove deep divisions between the two worlds. Yes, travellers were, and in many cases still are, secretive, but our ways are dying out and we want to protect and preserve them and the prejudices we face keep us marginalised to this day.

Things are changing, however. A few years ago I got a call out of the blue from a television company which was making a series called *Danny Dyer's Deadliest Men*. I'd never heard of Danny Dyer or the show but the programme producers knew about my reputation, thanks to the Internet. When I started fighting there was no such thing as computers or YouTube but as the years went on, footage of some of my fights had ended up on websites and the people making the series had seen them and read about my reputation. The more research they did into bare-knuckle fighting, the more my name came up. They wanted one of the shows to be about gypsies and they wanted me to feature in it.

At first I thought it was a wind-up. As far as I knew no traveller had been involved in a mainstream television series about fighting before. It was our secret world, why would country folk be interested? It's not as if they would understand. But the more I thought about it, the more I thought maybe it would be a good idea. We had nothing to hide and everything to prove.

A lot of people in the community thought it was a bad idea. Years of secrecy had made many people wary of country folk and they argued that shining the light of publicity on our ways could only lead to no good. They warned me against taking part. But the thing with me is, if you tell me not to do something I'll do it, just for the hell of it. So I agreed and Danny Dyer came to meet me at the Salford site with his film crew. He's known as a bit of a hard nut but I can tell you, when he walked onto the site he was shitting himself.

He interviewed me and I told him about traveller fighting ways and then I took him to Appleby fair. I thought it would be a bit of fun. It wasn't as if I was fighting any more. They filmed me for a couple of days, went away, edited it cleverly and put words in my mouth. I'd told them about the fighting I had done when I was younger but the show made out I was still fighting, even though I was almost 50 when it was filmed. Still, I enjoyed doing it and when the show came out, a lot of people thought it was a good thing.

Perhaps that show sparked some interest because a while later I was contacted again by another television company.

'The show is called what?' I had to double check.

'*My Big Fat Gypsy Wedding,*' said the man on the other end of the phone. It was a one-off Cutting Edge documentary for Channel 4 about traveller weddings and traveller life, he explained. I thought it was a fantastic idea. It would let people see a little more about our lives, how protective we are of our children, our morals and the way we are raised. Again people said I was mad to expose myself to public scrutiny. Even Roseanne said: 'Paddy, don't do this.'

But this show wasn't about fighting. It was a way for people to see that we are, on the whole, good, honest family people. I did it because it was something different and I could see that it might be a good thing.

The camera crew turned up and I had a great laugh doing it. I knew a few of the other travellers on the show.

I made sure I told everyone on the site what was going on and gave them all a few weeks' warning to make sure they were happy. If they weren't happy with it I wouldn't have done it. I explained what the show would be about and they trusted me. I wasn't about to lose that trust for the sake of a television show. I wasn't going to put that trust in jeopardy for the sake of people I didn't know.

The show came out and it blew the ocean up. I couldn't believe it. Country people had never got into travellers' circles before, they knew little of our culture and they got to see that we aren't as bad as they thought we were, we aren't the 'fucking pikeys' that most of us had been called all our lives. And we hate that word. Pikes are the dirtiest fish in the water; they eat anything and everything. People should realise that is not the right word for us. Before that word is used people should do their homework.

After *My Big Fat Gypsy Wedding* came out people tended to look at us in a different way, they were a bit more respectful. With Danny Dyer it was all about hard men and I didn't want to be recognised for that any more, I wanted to be recognised for me and the way I am. I have always been a family man. I love my children. The door of my trailer is always open to them and they take full advantage. They are in and out of it all day. I live on a site now with Simey, Margaret and Martin Tom. David and Johnny are always around. Whenever we can we sit down and eat together as a family and the phone never stops ringing. We know what each other is doing every second of the day.

After the show I got recognised. People would actually talk to me on the street, country people. It was lovely, instead of being reserved and standoffish people would approach me and strike up conversations. Then the series came out and it got even bigger. *My Big Fat Gypsy Wedding* changed the way people thought of travellers.

Within the traveller community there were still people who didn't like the publicity but the vast majority were for it and feel it has been a positive thing. You will always get naysayers and people who want to remain secretive but times move on. No matter how much people criticised it there was still a second series and more, so there are enough people wanting to take part and enough people interested enough to watch it. Millions of people watched it, which means that millions of people now understand more about who travellers are, and that can only be a good thing. Ironically, when they got in touch they told me what it was going to be called and I just started laughing, I thought it would go nowhere.

Suddenly, and without trying, I had become a minor personality. I didn't go looking for fame, it found me; I was offered a few opportunities and I took them for no other reason than I thought they might do some good and I like to do different things. But fame is a two-edged sword and I soon found out that the media can build you up and knock you down just as easily.

It began with an argument on the day of my sister Margaret's funeral in August 2010. It wasn't my argument, but as usual I got drawn in. It was between a sausage called Johnny Joyce, his brother and my son-in-law. They had a fight after the funeral and the Joyces split my brother-in-law's eye badly. It had nothing to do with me, young men are young men and these things happen, but I got involved and tried to calm the whole thing down. As far as I was concerned it was finished with there and then.

A week later I was out with a group of friends. I had been drinking all day and ended up in a club until about 2.30 a.m. when Johnny Joyce came in and out of the blue started speaking to me.

'You know that argument we had Paddy, it's forgotten isn't it?' he asked.

'Of course,' I said. 'I'm old school, it's water under the bridge.'

I asked him what he was drinking. He told me brandy and Coke and I got him one. He just sipped his drink while I was knocking them back and after the club we went back to my place.

I was rolling drunk by then and Roseanne gave me what for when I got home.

I invited Johnny back to my place. He came and at some point we started to have words. I can't remember what about but I do remember turning away from him. When I did he slipped on a heavy metal ring that covered three of his fingers and smashed me in the face. I was knocked out before I felt it. I was so drunk I was a sitting duck. While I was out cold he jumped on top of me and beat me for four minutes. I know it was that long because it happened outside my chalet and it was on CCTV.

My face was a mess. He shattered one side of my jaw in seven places, the other side in three and my chin in four places. He was 22 at the time, I was in my early fifties. When he finished he got off me and ran away.

Martin Tom found me unconscious on the floor in the same spot I'd been shot several years before. Once again the poor kid ran off to find Roseanne crying, 'I think Daddy's dead.'

I was lying in a pool of blood when my Roseanne found me. My son-in-law Johnny was in at the time and helped me into his car and drove me to the hospital. He didn't want to wait for an ambulance. By the time we got there I had come round but I couldn't speak. My mouth was so damaged my tongue was swelling like a balloon. It was closing my throat and I couldn't breathe. There and then the doctors cut my throat open to make an airway. My face was massive, there was blood everywhere. I was mumbling and in agony. I didn't think I was going to make it. With my hand free I blessed my face to God. Help me my

God, please save me, I said in my head and that was the last thing I remember.

I was sedated with painkillers and stitched up and put on a life-support machine to help me breathe. Later I was taken to Manchester Royal because there was a plastic surgery expert there. Roseanne couldn't believe it was me, my face was a mess and I had tubes coming out of me. Roseanne and my mother both called the police. The CID came to the hospital. I was in no fit state to talk to anyone but the doctors told them I might not make it so they went and cordoned off my home. They thought it could become a murder scene.

My cheekbones had gone and my eye sockets had caved in. The titanium plates in my jaw were crooked so they had to take them out and reset them. I had surgery to reconstruct my face. I came out of intensive care and went into a private ward. I remember waking up trying to shout but my jaw was wired up.

The next days were a haze of pain punctuated by morphine. At one point Roseanne was talking to me. I was livid because of the injustice of it. I had lived by the old ways: you fight, someone wins, you shake hands and that's it over. I had become firm friends with some of my fiercest opponents. But that wasn't the way any longer. Young men seemed to bear grudges, they couldn't let things go. And they fought dirty. I hadn't asked for trouble and I didn't want it.

Roseanne said: 'Paddy you have spent your whole life fighting, you have got to put this man away, he did this to you and you know him, what would he do to a stranger? You have to press charges.'

Initially I said no. Even though I had left those days behind me, I wanted to sort it out my way. Old habits die hard. But Roseanne persisted.

'I want you to swear on Patrick's grave that you will go to the police and get this man put away,' she said.

I was out of my head on morphine and said yes. I made a promise I couldn't break.

I was let out of hospital and stayed at home for several days, dosed up on painkillers. Roseanne begged me to go and make a statement and at first I refused. Then she reminded me that I swore on Patrick's grave. I was stuck between a rock and a hard place. I knew I couldn't go back on my word but I also knew that a lot of people would fall out with me because going to the police is not the travellers' way. But my word to my woman and my son meant more to me than the opinions of others so I told the police what happened and Johnny got arrested.

The case went to court and all the while we were waiting for it to be heard the papers were reporting it. Because of the TV shows I was suddenly big news.

I hated seeing myself in the papers. It shone a light on me and my family and we had no control over what was written. There were all kinds of misleading reports and Roseanne took the negative publicity very hard. The strain got so much for her she suffered a breakdown and threatened to kill herself. It turned our life upside down. Suddenly we were in the glare of publicity. At one point we had to leave the country just to get away from the constant newspaper reports. I hated myself for putting my wife in that situation. Suddenly we found out about the downside of fame. I never realised it was ruthless, the way they pick you and put you on a pedestal and then knock you down and walk over you. It's bad enough getting a beating but they beat you when you are down on the ground.

The reports that really hurt were the ones that said I was crying. I had never cried to anyone and I never backed down to anyone. They said I had gone running to the police. I hadn't. They said the two Joyce brothers were my cousins, they aren't cousins. They are also not travellers. They haven't lived in trailers. They think they are travellers but they are mongrels, neither travellers nor country people.

After *Big Fat Gypsy Weddings* I was one of the heroes, almost like an ambassador for travellers but then, within a few months, I was public enemy number one.

By the time the case came to court in February 2011 I didn't want to go and give evidence. I wanted nothing to do with it. In the stand I told the judge I didn't care if Joyce went to jail or not because I wasn't bothered about him. He got found not guilty of GBH. He pleaded self-defence.

25

Acceptance

I wish I could say that was it. I would have happily walked away and never set eyes on Johnny Joyce again. But the accusations continued to fly. There was bad blood between our families and the feud continued to simmer in the background, whether I was involved or not.

Four months after the court case, on a warm June afternoon I was jogging along the road in Salford with a friend. We were just on the last leg of a four-mile run when a car pulled up alongside us and the abuse started. I looked over, and Johnny Joyce and his brother Dougie were getting out of the car. We were on the main road outside a branch of PC World.

'You dirty Doherty bastard,' they were calling.

I'd never run away from anyone in my life and I wasn't about to then so I went over to them. There were two of them, they were both young men in their prime; I was 52 and had just finished a punishing run. I didn't intend on starting trouble, the odds were against me and I assumed that in the interests of fairness, the Joyces would have enough good sense not to attack me. It was a busy road and there were plenty of witnesses.

'You know who we are? We are the Joyces,' they said cockily, as if they had reputations to be proud of.

'I don't give a fuck who you are, you shitty bastards,' I said, 'you are nothing to me you bag of shit.'

Before I knew it Johnny cracked me in the face. He was wearing a ring and he caught me under the eye. The flesh opened up immediately.

He swung at me again and I had no choice but to defend myself. I was exhausted and there was hardly anything left in me after the run but I had no option but to square up to him and try and defend myself. As we went at each other his little brother started videoing the fight on his phone. He was shouting, 'Give it to the dirty bastard', egging his brother on. He had no shame. Eventually Johnny went down and I went down on top of him and we started grappling on the ground. Dougie stopped videoing and joined in. At one point one of them bit my ear so hard it was practically ripped off. It hung from my head by a piece of skin. I didn't feel pain, only anger and injustice. Their combined age still wouldn't add up to mine. In my day there would be no way that kids would be allowed to attack older men. If my sons ever did something like that I would be ashamed beyond words. When they finished Dougie, the dirty cowardly bastard, picked up his phone and took a photograph of me before they both ran off. I ended up in hospital again and my ear and eye had to be stitched up.

There were so many witnesses that before long the police were knocking on my door. Despite the fact that there were two of them and I was much older than they were, I was charged with affray. A few days after the fight I went to court and pleaded guilty. My barrister and family tried to persuade to plead not guilty and go to trial but I knew that would create a whole media circus and I couldn't put Roseanne through that again. It would have tipped her over the edge. I just wanted the matter to be over. If I went before a jury and pleaded my case I also figured I wouldn't get a fair hearing because of the prejudices people have towards travellers. Being charged with anything at all seemed to me to be a huge injustice so why should I expect fair play in a courtroom?

Outside the courtroom there was a brawl between our two clans. Six people were arrested. It had nothing to do with me, I was inside the courthouse but it confirmed to me that a long trial would have caused me and my family even more trouble. I went home and waited for a date to come through for my hearing.

It was in those weeks after the attack that my life took another bizarre turn. I was at home one evening relaxing in front of the television when the phone rang.

'Mr Doherty?' the person asked.

'Yes.'

'I'm phoning from the television company which makes *Big Brother*. We are doing a celebrity version in August and we'd like you to be on it.'

'Yeah, of course you do. Goodbye,' I said and hung up. I was convinced it was someone I knew having a wind up.

The phone rang again.

'Sorry, Mr Doherty, I think we got cut off, as I was saying I am calling from—'

I started to get angry.

'Joke over pal,' I said, 'don't call again.' I put the phone down.

Eventually though they did get through to me and arranged to send someone to see me. I thought it was a blast. Why on earth would anyone want me to go on *Big Brother*? I wasn't a celebrity; I was a traveller and a nobody, and travellers didn't go on *Big Brother*. Even when they turned up at the site in Salford I still thought it was a laugh but they said they would love to have me.

I thought they were mad but something about the madness of the idea made it appeal to me. What a craic; me mixing with celebrities for three weeks. I'd only seen bits and pieces of other *Celebrity Big Brother* shows but I knew enough to realise that they would chose people who might get on each other's nerves to cause a bit of friction and make good viewing.

I warned the television company. 'If someone gets contrary, I will tell them what I think of them,' I said.

They seemed more than happy with that and a few weeks later referred me to a psychiatrist. I sat in his office and told him straight.

'If someone tries to mess with me I won't put up with it,' I said.

By that time I had started to hear rumours about who else would be in the house and heard that the American singer Bobby Brown was going in. I also heard that he could be difficult.

'If Bobby Brown thinks he's going to put one on me I will knock him out before security gets to me,' I explained.

The psychiatrist asked me loads of questions. 'If someone hits you would you hit them back?'

'Of course,' I said. 'If someone treats me with respect I'll respect them back. If someone treats me bad I'll treat them bad. I might be a traveller but I am not there to be walked over.'

At the end of the session the man turned to me and said: 'Don't be surprised if you win it.'

'That's never going to happen in a million years,' I laughed.

I thought he was joking with me. I still thought the whole thing was a big joke, especially as there was a fee involved. I couldn't believe someone would pay me to go in a house and sit around. I assumed I'd only get a week before I was kicked out.

Roseanne and my old man were dead against it. Roseanne knew what had happened the last time I was on television and worried that the papers would tear me apart again, especially with the Joyce case hanging over me. She reckoned there would be so much jealousy that everyone would want to fight me when I came out.

'Why would they want to do that, I'm a man of age, I'm not into the fighting any more.' I told her. 'I'm getting a few quid, I'll only be in there a week and it's an achievement for a traveller just to get in there. People will look at me in a different light and I'll be home before you know it.'

I was so convinced I'd make boring viewing and get sent home that I never put a penny on myself. And in the beginning I was 57 to 1.

In the weeks leading up to the first day in the house I was on a roller coaster. I couldn't tell anyone what I was doing because it had to stay a secret and I didn't think of the implications. I was excited. There were meetings and plans and the weeks passed quickly. On 10 August 2011 I waved goodbye to Roseanne and my family, I gave my woman a kiss and said I'd see her in a week. I told her I loved her and caught a train to London.

The minute I sat on my own the realisation of what I was about to do hit me and my stomach churned. Up until that point it had been all systems go but suddenly I had a couple of hours to myself to contemplate what could go wrong. And I realised a lot of things were at stake. I started to imagine all the bad things that could happen. I was representing every traveller and if I looked bad or made a fool of myself, that would reflect on every traveller, every breed.

A few days before my father had said something to me. 'You are taking everyone on Patrick, you are taking our whole world on.' Suddenly I realised what he meant. What I did in that house would reflect on our whole world. What I was doing had never been done before. I was going to be scrutinised 24/7. To have that pressure was immense. The penny didn't just drop, it crashed through my skull and an hour into that journey I was thinking '*What have I done?*' It was 50/50 whether I jumped off at the next station.

When I got to Euston station in London I was met by people from the television company and whisked out the back door of the station so no one could see me. I was taken to a hotel and locked in a room on my own, then I was taken to a studio for a photoshoot. I was driven around in a car with blacked-out windows and whenever I went from car to building I had a blanket over my head so no one knew who I was. I felt like a freak. All the secrecy didn't help my feeling of unease. At that point the money became irrelevant. They could have given me a million pounds and I would have turned the opportunity down but by then it was too late.

That night I stayed in a hotel and didn't sleep a wink. The next day I went to the studios ready for the show to begin that evening and when the cameras started rolling so began three of the most infuriating and surreal weeks of my life.

The first person I saw in the house who I recognised was Kerry Katona. I only knew her from what I had seen in the papers and that wasn't too complimentary.

'Lovely,' I thought. 'Here's a girl who's game for a laugh.' She knew my name, put her arms around me and gave me a kiss. I was shocked she even knew who I was.

Next up was Amy Childs from *The Only Way Is Essex*. I'd never seen the show and I knew nothing about her. She truly was a diamond. I tried pushing the buttons with her a few times just to wind her up.

On the first night we were let into the bedroom and I clocked straight away that there were single and double beds. I was a happily married man and there was no way I was going to be forced into sharing a bed with any of the women. We all ran to stake a claim on a bed and I knocked Amy out of the way in the process. I knew the women would be making a play during the time we were in there because they were celebrities and they would want to be noticed so I let them know straight away that I was not up for any of that. I was right. In the nights they called out: 'Pad, can we have a cuddle?'

'Go and cuddle a pillow,' I'd call back.

If they came over to my bed I said: 'Don't even attempt to get in here, I'll knock you out.'

I never cuddled any of them or put my arms around them, they knew exactly how I felt.

On that first night I sat down and I couldn't believe how quickly I weighed them all up. I knew who was playing a game and who wanted all the attention. Amy loved the camera and the camera loved her because she is a beautiful woman. She had the manners of a princess, you rarely heard her swear. She's a kind-hearted girl. To me she's not fully grown up yet.

Kerry is a really nice person. But in my opinion she seems a little bit confused and misunderstood.

I knew what Bobby Sabel was the moment I looked at him. To me he seemed so vain although I hear he has denied it; a nice chap, but a sausage. I asked him what he did and he explained he was a model. I assumed if he was in there he would be a famous catwalk model but it turned out he was a catalogue model. I felt sorry for Lucien Laviscount because he appeared to want to be everyone's friend and if someone fell out with him he would do anything to get back in and be their friend again. He told me he was in *Corrie*. I watch it but I didn't recognise him.

The Jedwards played a game all the way through. They know that their career only has a short shelf life and that they only have a small window of opportunity to get away with acting like they do so they put it on as much as they can. After two weeks they went quiet because they ran out of steam. I was watching them all the time.

My main man in the house, and one of the loveliest country men I've met, was Mr Paparazzi, Darryn Lyons. I knew nothing about him when I met him but he was a man's man. What you see is what you get with him. If you didn't like him he wasn't bothered. If you liked him he would like you back. He was like me, totally straight and not playing any games.

The two Americans, Tara Reid and Pamela Bach, appeared to be away with the fairies. They were actors and they acted all day long.

And then there was Sally Bercow, the wife of the Speaker of the House of Commons. When I first saw Sally I knew she was playing no games. I asked someone who she was and they said she was the Speaker's wife. I didn't know who or what the Speaker was. Then she spoke and I loved her voice. She made out she was rough but she wasn't. She was what we travellers call a horse of a different colour, she wasn't what she made herself out to be, and me and her ended up having many interesting conversations. She knew the buttons to press and tried to get a reaction from me. I liked her for that

'Your son could be gay,' she said to me one day.

'Hey woman, don't be saying that,' I told her. 'My son is a true stallion.'

I thought she was playing me but she wasn't. One day she invited me to the Houses of Parliament and I thought, 'Not in a million years, she's just saying it for the cameras.' I said, 'Have I got your word?' and she gave me her word and backed it right up. She was very blunt, that's her downfall. She came across as judgemental sometimes but she's a good woman.

She was surprised by the way I spoke about Roseanne. She asked if I cleaned at home and I told her the truth, that I did nothing.

'I tell you what I do,' I explained. 'I service my woman.'

Sally is so posh she didn't know what I meant. When she found out she was offended because she's into woman's lib.

'That wasn't a good thing you said to me about your wife, Paddy,' she said.

'But I do service her,' I replied. 'Don't worry, I wouldn't service you.'

I made a decision when I went in the house to be myself. I wasn't going to hide anything or apologise for who or what I am. Everyone has their own opinions about travellers and the way our women live but that is the way travellers have been brought up for generations and I wasn't going to deny that cleaning is a way of life for traveller women; if they want to do something else, good luck to them. If Roseanne wanted to do something different, I'd be behind her. Ultimately I don't care what people think, the main thing is that my woman is happy with what she is doing and I know she is. I wouldn't have the bad manners to criticise someone else's way of life. Opinions are like arseholes: everyone has them but they should be kept private.

After a few days I began to realise how much I hated being in a house. I hadn't lived in one since I left my mother's and I felt some days like the walls were closing in on me. Freedom is the one thing that travellers prize above everything else. If you gave me a mansion I would swap it for a bit of land and a trailer.

All my life I have been able to take off when the mood takes me, but in there I was stuck with the same faces day in day out. The boredom got to me the most. Viewers see the highlights for an hour a night and it looks like there is lots going on but for each hour of excitement there were 23 hours of boredom. I found being in a fishbowl environment stressful. It made me start smoking. I was smoking like a trooper by the end of it.

It wasn't long before the Jedwards really started to get on my nerves. One evening we were allowed to watch a film. I thought they said it was a great fighting film, which would have suited me fine. I thought it was *Rocky* or something. What they actually said was a great *frightening* film. I hate horror movies. I can't watch them. I get terrified. My grandchildren threaten me with the video of *Bride of Chucky* when they are blackguarding me. I was sitting there watching the movie and I wanted a doctor to see to my stomach and a priest to give me a blessing I was that terrified. To make matters worse it was in 3D. The Jedwards were behind me making *woo* noises and Bobby was trying to wind me up. At that point I really was ready to go for him and the twins. Was working out how much damage I could have done before the minders arrived. I think Bobby could see I was serious because he backed off. He'll never know how close he was to getting a dig on live television. And I would have drowned the Jedwards.

By the end of the movie I couldn't get out the door fast enough. I went to the diary room and I had the shakes. I asked for tablets to calm me down. I told them I was going to commit three murders out there and they kept me in the diary room for three hours to calm me down. They gave me tablets and I don't know what they were but when I came out I was as calm as a kitten.

I missed my Roseanne every day I was there and I'd go into the diary room regularly to ask if she was okay. On the outside the TV company made sure they kept in contact with her. It was the longest I'd ever been away from her, in all the years we had been married we had rarely been apart and I was surprised by how much I missed her. The days I could handle, but at night it was so lonely.

After a week I'd had enough and I went into the diary room to ask to leave. I wanted to pick up my money and go home. But the producers had a knack of talking people round and they persuaded me to stay.

I was still wary all the way through of making a fool of myself. There were a few times when I did think it had gone too far. I had to dress up as a dog for one task and I really didn't want to do it. The crew talked me into it but I felt so degraded.

There were plenty of laughs though and I made some good friends in there, Sally and Darryn especially. By the last week even the Jedwards had grown on me.

One day we were in the garden and Darryn took his top off. I did a double take. He had the most defined set of abs I'd ever seen. I was fascinated; I kept following him everywhere to look at them.

'Are they for real? How can you get them like that?' I asked.

He told me they were false. They looked the dog's bollocks, I'd never seen anything like them in my life.

When I first went in I thought it would be impossible for me to win. I never agreed to go in because I wanted to be popular. At first I agreed for the simple reason that I saw it as a dare and a challenge and all my life I had never ducked out of a contest. I also knew what a big deal it was for a traveller to be asked to take part in such a big show and in my own small way I wanted to further some of the goodwill and understanding between country people and travellers that *Big Fat Gypsy Weddings* had already started. I wasn't in it for the fame and I certainly wasn't in it for the fortune.

So when the three weeks came to an end and the final night rolled around I was looking forward to being one of the first people out of the house and seeing my family again. I was anxious because I still had no idea how I had been perceived on the outside. We really had been locked away from everything and had no clue what had been going on in the outside world.

I assumed the contest would be between the Jedwards, Kerry and Amy because they were the most famous and would have the most fans voting for them. Bobby wasn't going to win. Neither was Lucien and I knew the Americans were going early as well. As each housemate began to leave I told myself that if I beat Amy I would be happy; that would be a big result. We were voted off one by one and when Amy went I was thrilled with myself. I still had no thoughts about winning and I assumed either me or Kerry would be next to go and the Jedwards would win. When their name was called out I was shocked. I looked in their eyes and saw they were crestfallen. They were desperate to win. That left me and Kerry. At that point the realisation sunk in. There was a real possibility that I could be the last in.

Kerry turned to me.

'You'll win Paddy,' she said. I knew she wanted it so badly and I hoped she was wrong because it meant less to me than it did to her. 'Who am I,' I thought, 'I'm just a gypsy.'

It happened so fast I have to watch it back to remind myself. There I was, on the sofa with Kerry, she was clutching and stroking my arm and bloody Brian Dowling was stretching out the moment before he announced the winner of the competition. The anticipation was unbearable, but I still thought I wasn't going to win. Not in my heart of hearts. I was ready to turn round and congratulate Kerry. And then Brian called out my name.

I was astonished, I put my hands to my head in amazement. What had just happened? Had I heard correctly? Had the country folk of Great Britain really just crowned me, a traveller, a gypsy, the winner of *Big Brother*?

I leapt up out of the sofa and gave Kerry a hug. Bless her, she seemed genuinely pleased that I had won. I swung her around, and as I shouted in joy and amazement, Brian said, 'Paddy, I think you're happy.' And I was. Happy and amazed that people had watched me, saw who I was, and voted for me. I didn't care about winning, what mattered to me was that it was proof that attitudes had changed so much that a gypsy could win a national popularity contest. Suddenly it seemed like the world had accepted me and my people.

When I walked out the house the crowd went wild. I had never heard anything like it. The hairs on the back of my neck stood up. There was a sea of people and all of them were cheering and chanting my name. People were holding up home-made placards that they had made especially for me. Strangers had done this, people who I didn't know had watched me and cared enough about me to turn up and cheer my departure from the house as winner of *Big Brother*. I choked up. The goodwill and love that poured from these people was incredible, you could feel it in the air. As a traveller, you spend your life being different from country folk, you're constantly justifying how you live and who you are. But this felt like acceptance, not just of Paddy Doherty the man, but also of Paddy Doherty, the gypsy.

It was one of the greatest feelings of my life.

26

One Last Fight

'Where's my woman?' I was scanning the faces in the crowd. The noise and the cheers were deafening. Brian Dowling, the presenter, was talking to me but I wasn't listening. I just wanted to see Roseanne. If she was there, everything would be okay. If she wasn't there I would be off, no interviews, no nothing.

I needed to make sure she was happy. I still didn't know how I had come across: whether I had won because people liked me or because I was a national joke. I needed to know that I hadn't humiliated Roseanne.

I was taken into the studio and I saw my kids, Margaret, Davey and Simey.

'Where's your mum?' I mouthed.

Then I saw her standing behind them. She was smiling and she looked lovely. I knew from the look on her face that everything was going to be fine and I allowed myself to relax a little and I did the interviews and photos. In the early hours of the morning I went to a hotel room with my family. I could hardly sleep that night, I was still full of adrenaline and my mind was turning over. I couldn't believe what had happened and there was still a nagging worry in my head that maybe I had dishonoured my people in some way.

The next day the calls started. My brothers Hughie, Johnny and Simey called to congratulate me and tell me what a great thing I had done. When I heard that I thanked God that it hadn't backfired. Then fighting men such as Bobby Frankham and Bobby Butcher called and commended me for what I'd done for the traveller community. Then I heard from the heads of the big families: the Rooneys, the Cashs, the Coyles. I got calls from my people in Ireland; the Quinn McDonaghs, the McGuires and the O'Donnells. All of them told me they were proud of me. The relief and the honour I felt was overwhelming. I was walking on the moon. The realisation of what I'd done started to fully sink in. In my lifetime I had achieved something that I didn't think possible. I'd shown the world that travellers are good decent people and that we are human beings just like everyone else. For that I know my name will always be remembered by my people and that is a huge honour.

When I got back home on Sunday all I wanted to do was get in the chalet and lock myself away. I just needed to gather my thoughts and have some quiet time. It felt good to be back in a trailer. My plans for a quiet night did not work out. Everyone came over and a party broke out.

There was sad news as well as good. When I came out I learnt that one of my good friends from Salford had been shot in the back and killed in a pub. Lee Erdman was one of the men I knew from the gym. I had known him and his brothers for many years and they trained with my sons. They were like brothers and Lee was good man. It was a tragedy and a waste of life. It brought home to me how I was at a point in my life where I was standing between two worlds; my past and present.

As things began to settle down over the following days I started to realise that when I left the *Big Brother* house, I left a part of me in there. My life was changing and it would never be the same. I had to start thinking about things like signing an agent. I didn't know what an agent was or what an agent did but I was advised to get one. I had no idea how the world of celebrity worked and didn't see myself as one. It was a world that was totally alien to me and it was both exciting and confusing at the same time.

I started to get invited to celebrity parties and film premieres. I wasn't bothered about that fake world but I did start to realise I could use my name for good. I could do charity work. I attended charity balls and at one I heard that Brad Pitt wants to make a film about me.

'Does he now?' I said, laughing.

I found myself in situations I could never have dreamed about. I was a rough fighting gypsy but a few months after *Big Brother* I found myself in the House of Commons, shaking hands and having a craic with the Speaker, John Bercow, one of the most powerful and respected men in the country. Sally had made good on the promise she had made to me in the house and introduced me to her husband.

I vowed never to forget my past and never to change the person I was because I am proud of who I am and where I came from. My court case hung over me. There were the usual headlines in the papers as the sentencing date approached: 'Paddy's jail fears', 'Paddy Whacked'. I learnt to ignore them but each time there was a story Roseanne would get anxious and I'd get calls all day from friends and family asking if I was going to jail. Eventually the court case came and I was given a suspended sentence. A few weeks later the Joyce brothers were sentenced. Dougie was given 150 hours' community service; Johnny was jailed for 15 months. It should have been longer. Since then I've bought two asses that I keep in a field near my home. They are lazy, ugly, good-for-nothing animals but they entertain the children, so I call them Dougie and Johnny.

I moved from Salford too. I loved the area and the people there but after the shooting and the Joyce attack I had mixed memories about the site. It was time for a change. I now live in North Wales on a smaller site.

I also gave up being a fair play man. It was too hard for me to do. I'd become too well known and I'd bring attention to something that still remains a confidential part of my culture. If I turned up to a fight to show fair play it would cause more harm than good. I retired from fighting altogether. Making that decision was hard; fighting is in my blood and the life and breath of the community I love. But I had to do it for the good of my people. And anyway, I had a much bigger battle on my hands...

Call me a dreamer, but after *Big Brother* I really believed that perhaps things had changed between travellers and country folk. There was a level of understanding that had never been there when I was growing up.

Thanks to television, both communities had a bit of common ground. I can't say that all the old prejudices have gone, there will always be people who will never mix on both sides, but at least country people have been able to see that while travellers live different lives, we are still people with families and hopes and loves and dreams.

But then there was Dale Farm.

Dale Farm is a plot of land in Essex. Originally, from the 1960s, it was used as a scrapyard. In recent decades it had been owned by travellers and pitches started being placed on it in the eighties. Right next door there is an authorised site for 40 trailers. In 2001, the site was sold to a traveller and more trailers were pitched on it. Since being used as a scrapyard the land had always been used for industry and for periods it was disused, just sitting there, unoccupied. Over the years, as travellers were forced into permanent camps, it became a place to bring up families and there was a sense of community there.

But after a protracted ten-year legal battle, the council finally won the right to throw the families out. It became huge news and camera crews were permanently stationed outside the gates of the site reporting on the eviction proceedings. I wonder how much attention the families on Dale Farm would have received from the outside world had *Big Fat Gypsy Weddings* and *Celebrity Big Brother* not happened?

The families were being evicted on the grounds of contravening planning permission; something big corporations get away with all the time. Because of who they were the Dale Farm residents were subject to the same prejudices travellers have faced for years: they were dirty, they were scroungers, they were lowering house prices and destroying the middle-class way of life. But that's not true. Travellers keep themselves to themselves and don't mess about in country folks' business. The gypsies at Dale Farm were using a piece of land that had been used for scrap before they came along – and it seemed that some country folk would have preferred a scrapyard on their doorstep to families going about their business.

I don't know if I'm a celebrity, but I do know that I'm probably one of the most famous travellers at the moment, and if I can use that to help my people, that's all to the good. I reckoned that my position came with a degree of responsibility to speak up for my people and so I went on television to defend them.

'I'm a traveller until I die, until God takes me from this earth. They tried to take our place away – Dale Farm. They should find a bit of land and say, "There you are, that's yours." Please, treat them like human beings, not dirt,' I told reporters.

Going on site there was a real feeling of anger, but also of community. The travellers were going to stand together on this one. But it wasn't just travellers, there were country folk protesting as well – one country woman even locked her neck to the gates, which meant that she would be killed if the bailiffs tried to open them.

But on 19 October 2011, the protest failed and the police moved in. The council had won and over 400 people were moved off site. Some went peacefully; some had to be removed by force. These were people who had children in the nearby school and who had built homes for themselves. Their homes were bulldozed. It was ethnic cleansing. I saw kids crying and was taken back to my own traumatic days of being bullied at school. It made my heart ache. I still have trouble understanding why it happened. In the last fifty years there has been increasing pressure on travellers to settle on permanent camps. There are fewer and fewer places for us to travel to and the government makes a show of providing sites. But in the case of Dale Farm, when families do decide to settle, they are thrown off and treated like criminals. It doesn't make sense.

It was a sad day when I heard the news that Dale Farm had been cleared. Perhaps us travellers weren't as close to being accepted by country folk as I had thought.

I am who I am. I don't make excuses, why should I have to? I make no apologies for my life. I love my family and I'll always do whatever it takes to protect them. I am very proud of who I am and what I am. I teach my children to be proud too. Because being a traveller means everything to me. It's not just a label, it goes much deeper. It's an identity that is burned into my heart.

In my time I've been known as a hard man, as a fighting man. My days of violence are gone now but my name goes before me and today I'm a fighter of a different kind. I fight for what I believe in: my family and my way of life. So-called celebrity and the things that go with it, they're all very nice but they can be gone in a flash. Celebrity means nothing. What you are and who you share your life with is the most important thing, and travellers know that. I'm a traveller, I'm proud to be a traveller and I wouldn't be anything else in the world.

Acknowledgements

Thank you to my woman, Roseanne, to all my children and to my mother and father.

Thank you to all the traveller families everywhere and to everyone who voted for me on *Celebrity Big Brother*.

Thank you to Kelly Ellis and the team at Ebury, my agent Chrissy, and thanks to my friend Nick Harding for your help and guidance.

And, lastly, thanks to Bobby Butcher and his lovely wife; God rest her.

About the Author

Born in 1959, Paddy Doherty is an Irish traveller and a former bare-knuckle boxer. He is most well-known for starring in hit Channel 4 show *My Big Fat Gypsy Wedding*. In 2011, he won *Celebrity Big Brother* and since then he has starred in his own reality TV series *When Paddy Met Sally* with Sally Bercow. He has been married to his wife Roseanne for over 34 years. The couple now live in a chalet in North Wales and have five surviving children and 15 grandchildren

Cent
15/09/20